ENGLISH LITERATURE
for AQA B

Tony Childs
Jackie Moore

Heinemann Educational Publishers,
Halley Court, Jordan Hill, Oxford OX2 8EJ
A division of Reed Educational & Professional Publishing Ltd

OXFORD MELBOURNE AUCKLAND
JOHANNESBURG BLANTYRE GABORONE
IBADAN PORTSMOUTH NH (USA) CHICAGO

First published 2000

2004 2003 2002 2001 2000
10 9 8 7 6 5 4 3 2 1

ISBN 0 435 10979 0

Acknowledgements

The publishers would like to thank the following for permission to use copyright material:
Extract from 'Animal Farm' by George Orwell Copyright © George Orwell 1945. Reproduced by permission of A. M. Heath & Co. Ltd. On behalf of Bill Hamilton as the Literary Executor of the Estate of the Late Sonia Brownell Orwell and Martin Secker & Warburg Limited; Extracts from 'Passage to India' and 'A Room With A View' by E. M. Forster. Reprinted by permission of The Provost and Scholars of King's College, Cambridge, and The Society of Authors as the literary representatives of the E. M. Forster Estate; Extract from 'The Color Purple' by Alice Walker, published in Great Britain by the Women's Press Ltd., 1983. Reprinted by permission of David Higham Associates Limited; Extract from 'Stopping by Woods On A Snowy Evening' from 'The Poetry of Robert Frost', edited by Edward Connery Lathem, published by Jonathan Cape. Reprinted with permission of Random House Group Limited on behalf of the estate of Robert Frost; Extract from 'The Virgin and the Gypsy' by D. H. Lawrence. Reprinted by permission of Laurence Pollinger Limited, on behalf of the Estate of Frieda Lawrence Ravagli; Extract from 'Hard Frost' from 'Selected Poems' by Andrew Young, published by Carcanet Press Limited. Reprinted by permission of Carcanet Press Limited; Extract from 'The Bonfire of the Vanities' by Tom Wolfe, published by Jonathan Cape, reprinted by permission of the Random House Group Limited; Extract from 'One Flew Over The Cuckoo's Nest' by Ken Kesey, published by Marion Boyars Publishers Limited. Reprinted by permission of Marion Boyars Publishers Limited; Extract from 'Sons and Lovers' by D. H. Lawrence. Reprinted by permission of Laurence Pollinger Limited, on behalf of the Estate of Frieda Lawrence Ravagli; Extracts from 'Things Fall Apart' by Chinua Achebe, published by Heinemann Educational. Reprinted with permission of the publishers; Extract from 'The Great Gatsby' by F. Scott Fitzgerald, published by Bodley Head. Reprinted by permission of David Higham Associates Limited; Extract from 'The Last Resort' by Alison Lurie, published by Chatto & Windus. Reprinted by permission of the Random House Group Limited; Extract from 'Down and Out in Paris and London' by George Orwell Copyright © George Orwell 1933. Reproduced by permission of A. M. Heath & Co. Ltd. On behalf of Bill Hamilton as the Literary Executor of the Estate of the Late Sonia Brownell Orwell and Martin Secker & Warburg Limited; Extract from 'Birdsong' by Sebastian Faulks, published by Vintage 1994. Reprinted by permission of Gillon Aitken Associates Limited; Extract from 'Mrs. Dalloway' by Virginia Woolf. Reprinted by permission of The Society of Authors as the literary representatives of the Estate of Virginia Woolf; Extracts from 'The Bell' and 'The Sea, The Sea' by Iris Murdoch, published by Chatto and Windus. Reprinted by permission of Random House Group Limited; Extract from 'The Long Finish' by Michael Dibdin, published by Faber and Faber Limited. Reprinted by permission of Faber and Faber Limited; Extract from 'Enduring Love' by Ian McEwan, published by Jonathan Cape. Reprinted by permission of the Random House Group Limited; Extract from 'The Knowledge of Angels' by Jill Paton Walsh, published by Transworld. Reprinted by permission of David Higham Associates Limited; Extract from 'The Bell Jar' by Sylvia Plath, published by Faber and Faber Limited. Reprinted by permission of Faber and Faber Limited; Extract from 'The Pangs of Love and other stories' by Jane Gardam, published by Chatto and Windus. Reprinted by permission of David Higham Associates Limited; Extract from 'The Go-Between' by L. P. Hartley (Hamish Hamilton 1953) copyright © by L. P. Hartley. This edition copyright © Douglas Brook Davies, 1997. Reprinted by permission of Penguin Books Limited; Extract from 'Death in Summer' by William Trevor (Viking 1998) copyright © William Trevor 1998. Reprinted by permission of Penguin Books Limited; Extract from 'A Child in Time' by Ian McEwan, published by Jonathan Cape. Reprinted by permission of the Random House Group Limited; Extracts from 'Catch-22' by Joseph Heller, Copyright © Joseph Heller 1955, published by Random House Group Limited. Reprinted by permission of A. M . Heath & Co Ltd; Extract from 'Behind the Scenes at the Museum' by Kate Atkinson © Kate Atkinson 1995, published by Black Swan, a division of Transworld Publishers. All rights reserved; Extract from 'Beloved' by Toni Morrison, published by Random House Group Limited. Copyright © Toni Morrison 1987. Reprinted by permission of International Creative Management Inc.; Extract from 'Cat's Eye' by Margaret Atwood, published by Bloomsbury in 1989. Reprinted by permission of Bloomsbury Publishing Plc.; Extract from 'Educating Rita' by Willy Russell, published by Methuen Publishing Limited. Reprinted by permission of Methuen Publishing Limited; Extract from 'Top Girls' by Caryl Churchill, published by Methuen Publishing Limited. Reprinted by permission of Methuen Publishing Limited; Extracts from 'Man for all Seasons' published by Heinemann Educational. Reprinted by permission of the publishers; Extracts from 'A Streetcar Named Desire' by Tennessee Williams. Copyright © 1947, 1953, renewed 1975, 1981 The University of the South, published by New Directions. Reprinted by permission of The University of the South, Sewanee, Tennessee; Extracts from 'Waiting for Godot' by Samuel Beckett, published by Faber and Faber Limited. Reprinted by permission of Faber and Faber Limited.

The publishers have made every effort to trace the copyright holders, but if they have inadvertently overlooked any, they will be pleased to make the necessary arrangements at the first opportunity.

Typeset by TechType, Abingdon, Oxon

Printed and bound by Bath Press in the UK

Contents

Introduction

How this book will help you

This book is designed to help students following AQA Specification B in Advanced Subsidiary English Literature through their course. It isn't a guide to individual set texts – after all, each of you will choose different texts to work on. Rather, it's a guide to what you must do with your texts in order to succeed.

This introduction deals with the Assessment Objectives for Specification B. Assessment Objectives are statements of what candidates – you – are tested on in any examination specification. Don't overlook this section and go straight to the modules. The Assessment Objectives underpin all the work in the course, and an understanding of them is the key to gaining good marks. Remember that the marking is based entirely on them.

The rest of the book deals with each of the three assessment modules for the course. For each module, we take you through its design and content with practical advice and activities. The work you're asked to do will be tailored to the type of assessment involved in the module; this might be external assessment – either open or closed book – or coursework. We also provide examples of the sorts of questions and tasks that will be used to test each module as part of the examination.

You will find a glossary for the book on pages 141–144.

The key to success: understanding the Assessment Objectives

Here are the Assessment Objectives for AS English Literature:

The examination will assess a candidate's ability to:
AO1 communicate clearly the knowledge, understanding and insight appropriate to literary study, using appropriate terminology and accurate and coherent written expression
AO2i respond with knowledge and understanding to literary texts of different types and periods
AO3 show detailed understanding of the ways in which writers' choices of form, structure and language shape meanings
AO4 articulate independent opinions and judgements, informed by different interpretations of literary texts by other readers
AO5i show understanding of the contexts in which literary texts are written and understood

As you can see, the Assessment Objectives define the literary skills that you must show in the course.

It is vital to understand that they carry different numbers of marks in different modules. For example, in Module 3, the Shakespeare coursework module, the 30 marks available are divided like this: AO1 5 marks, AO2i 5 marks, AO3 0 marks, AO4 15 marks and AO5i 5 marks. This means that half the marks for the module are awarded for showing 'an ability to articulate independent opinions and judgements, informed by different interpretations of literary texts by other readers'. On the other hand, there are no marks for showing 'detailed understanding of the ways in which writers' choices of form, structure and language shape meanings'.

So the marks depend on the Assessment Objectives and are awarded differently in each module. That's why we have provided boxes at the beginning of each of the three modules to show you exactly which Assessment Objectives count in that module and how many marks each one carries.

What the Assessment Objectives mean

Assessment Objective 1

This Assessment Objective is tested in each module, so it's really important. It requires you to be able to do three things:

> AO1   communicate clearly the knowledge, understanding and insight appropriate to literary study, using appropriate terminology and accurate and coherent written expression

- Make sure that what you write is legible and that spelling, grammar and punctuation are accurate, so that your meaning is clear.

- Acquire appropriate literary terminology, so that you can express your opinions about literary texts precisely and clearly. You already know many terms, but during the course you'll come across many more. You must understand these terms if you are to use them effectively in your writing; there is a glossary at the back of this book to help you.

- Construct clear and logical arguments. This is an important part of communicating clearly and being coherent. Whatever task you undertake in the course, it's important to sequence your response effectively – which means planning it carefully.

Assessment Objective 2i

> AO2i respond with knowledge and understanding to literary texts of different types and periods

This means that you must be able to:

- Show your knowledge of the text you're studying. Details of the text, quotations from it, echoes of it, would all show knowledge.

- Show your understanding of the texts you are studying. You can demonstrate this by the way you write about the ideas in the text – your view of the writer's ideas and concerns, and what you think about them.

- Study texts of different types and periods. This is actually ensured by the specification, which requires that for AS Level: you must study at least four texts; you must study one each of prose, poetry and drama, and also one play by Shakespeare; and you must choose one text, other than Shakespeare, which was published before 1900. The texts you have to choose from in Modules 1, 2 and 3 meet this part of the Objective.

Assessment Objective 3

> AO3 show detailed understanding of the ways in which writers' choices of form, structure and language shape meanings

This Objective requires you to:

- Show an understanding of writers' choices of form, and why they chose to use them.

In prose, for example, the writer's first choice of form was probably whether to write a novel or a short story. The writer may have chosen to write in first person or third person or a mixture, perhaps, and might have used different types of prose within the text, such as diaries or letters. The book might be of a recognisable type – an **allegory**, say, or a horror novel – and may or may not conform to the form characteristic of this type. What is the effect of some of these choices? Why did the writer make them?

In poetry, the poet may have chosen to write stanzas, or not. There might be a strict rhyme scheme, perhaps in a traditional form such as a sonnet, or blank verse or free verse. If there's a definite rhythm, it might stay the same throughout the poem or it might vary. If it varies, why did the poet choose this approach, and what effect does it have?

In drama, you might be looking at verse drama, or not. Shakespeare mostly wrote his plays in verse but used prose as well; you could look at why he chose to have particular passages in prose rather than verse. Is the play you're studying divided into acts and scenes? Why, or why not? Is the play in dialogue throughout, or are there any monologues? What are the effects of these choices?

- Show an understanding of the effects of writers' choices of structure.

In prose, for example, the novel or story could be written chronologically, or instead could employ time shifts such as flashbacks. If these shifts occur in a systematic way, can you identify the pattern and suggest their effect on the reader? Perhaps it's important to the novelist to reveal things at a certain point, or to set certain events or ideas against each other.

There are many other structural considerations. Are the chapters organised in a particular way, and do they begin or end in a way that reveals a pattern? Are there passages or chapters that don't advance the plot but give information vital for the reader, and if so, do they form a pattern? In poetry, the structure might be shown through the way the stanzas are organised. You'll also look at how the poem ends. Does it have a concluding thought, a universal thought, or a change of mood, for example? How does the poem prepare the reader for this ending? When you've read several poems by the same poet, as you will during Module 2, you may start to see uses of structures that are characteristic of the poet.

Some of these ideas about prose and poetry apply to drama too, such as why acts and scenes begin and end in the way they do, and why they're ordered in a particular way. A dramatist may use a sub-plot to provide another angle on one of the ideas in the piece; if so, how is it built into the structure, and what are its effects?

- Show an understanding of the effect of writers' choices of language.

Linguistic choices in prose, for example, have many purposes, as when 'I' and 'my' are used to establish a first-person narrator. Writers may choose to vary tense for a particular effect – a sudden switch from past to present to produce a feeling of immediacy is an obvious example. All sorts of patterns of words or **imagery** might appear in a novel to create atmosphere or meanings. If an authorial voice appears in the text, how is it shown through language?

'Poetic' language isn't just used in poetry – imagery, for instance, can be used effectively in prose and drama. However, poetry tends to be a more intense form so we might expect to find more language devices concentrated together. And the reverse is also true – a poet can choose to use very plain, simple language in a poem to create a particular effect.

In some ways, the language of drama is no different from that of poetry and prose. You might look for language that is plain or heightened, formal or informal, and so on – and at the reasons for the choices. But drama is written to be performed rather than read, so the audience hear the words only once. In order to create realistic characters on stage – if that is what the playwright wants to do – he or she chooses language that creates particular and different characters. The language may also try to capture the words and rhythms of speech in the context of the setting of the play, including overlapping speech.

• Show how the writers' choices shape meanings in the texts

The important thing for meeting this Assessment Objective is to recognise the relationship between means and purposes – not just the methods the writers choose, but why they use them. It's worth noticing that the Assessment Objective mentions 'meanings' rather than 'meaning'. A particular use of form, structure or language may create several possible meanings, not just one. For instance, here's a line from *The Tempest*:

> PROSPERO: Heavens rain grace on that which breeds between 'em.

The words 'rain' and 'breeds', combined in the same sentence and by the direct link suggested, are bound to make the audience think about fertility in some way. This is how the writer's choice has expressed a meaning. But the line is also open to other interpretations (AO4). It expresses Prospero's hope that the young couple's relationship will develop well. The audience may also reflect on what it tells them about Prospero and his attitude to power; about his intentions in the play, including revenge or forgiveness; and about what the couple might represent. There are also contexts (AO5) to think about. 'Grace' is a key word, and the concept of grace a key idea, in Shakespeare's last plays.

Assessment Objective 4

> AO4 articulate independent opinions and judgements, informed by different interpretations of literary texts by other readers

There are two main things to think about here. They affect the way you need to think about your texts and how you'll be tested on them. And remember that one informs the other – they cannot be tackled separately.

• 'articulate independent opinions and judgements'

Ambiguity and uncertainty are central to the reading of texts. Examination tasks expect candidates to take part in genuine critical enquiry, and teachers and examiners who assess your responses will not work to a 'right' answer they've got and you haven't. It's your overview and judgement, and the way you go about it, that will be assessed. This means that you must be confident enough in your knowledge and understanding of the text to form a clear personal and independent judgement about what it means to you.

• 'informed by different interpretations of literary texts by other readers'

The central premise here is that there is no single interpretation of any literary text. Readers of texts are all different, because everybody is affected by their own experiences and background. The way we interpret texts and their meanings can depend on who we are, and the way we've come to read them. In the same way, literary texts may be understood differently in different historical periods, and by different social groups.

Texts are bound to embody the attitudes and values of their writers, who in turn may embody the attitudes and values of a particular society or social group. They do not reflect an external, objective reality. Reality is different for different people at different times. In a way, all books are rewritten and reinterpreted by the societies that read them.

There are particular approaches and theories that suggest different ways of looking at texts, such as feminist, Marxist and Freudian ways of reading the text. You'll need to understand some critical concepts and terminology before you can think and write about these theories, so we offer some guidance in a later section of the book.

Assessment Objective 5i

> AO5i show understanding of the contexts in which literary texts are written and understood

There are many contextual frames surrounding literary texts – that is to say, many facts and processes shape the way a text is written. Here are some of the important types of relevant context:

- The period or era, including significant social, historical, political and cultural factors. This applies both to the period in which a text is set and the (perhaps different) period in which it is written.

- The writer's biography and/or milieu.

- Other works, including those by the same author. For example, you could look at the way Shakespeare's concerns in the last plays are presented in different plays.

- The work's different reception over time, including the recognition that works have different meanings and effects upon readers in different periods.

- A specific passage set against the work from which it is taken – a part-to-whole context. For example, choose a scene in a play and consider how it relates to the rest of the play in terms of structure, mood, language, etc.

- The literary environment, including generic factors and period-specific styles. For instance, you could examine a Restoration comedy in the light of the stage and comedy conventions of the day, and how the text conforms to them.

- The language used, including relevant and significant episodes in the use and development of literary language. This might include matters of style, such as the use of **colloquial, dialect** or **demotic** language.

Combining the Assessment Objectives

The Assessment Objectives are often intertwined, and become more so as you advance in your studies. Here is an example:

> What do you think Jane Austen has to say about virtue and vice in *Mansfield Park*? How does she present her ideas?

This question draws on four of the five Assessment Objectives (the presentation of your answer should also embody AO1, of course):

AO2i: You demonstrate your knowledge and understanding of the novel and what it has to say about virtue and vice;

AO3: You describe how Austen presents her ideas to make us understand what she has to say;

AO4: You apply independent judgement and interpretation to answer the 'What do you think . . . ' question successfully;

AO5i: You identify the relevant contexts for the novel as those of society and morality.

The Assessment Objectives for this module require that you:

ASSESSMENT OBJECTIVES

AO1 communicate clearly the knowledge, understanding and insight appropriate to literary study, using appropriate terminology and accurate and coherent written expression
(10% of the final AS mark; 5% of the final A Level mark)

AO2i respond with knowledge and understanding to a literary text
(5% of the final AS mark; 2½% of the final A Level mark)

AO3 show detailed understanding of the ways in which writers' choices of form, structure and language shape meanings
(10% of the final AS mark; 5% of the final A Level mark)

AO4 articulate independent opinions and judgements, informed by different interpretations of literary texts by other readers
(5% of the final AS mark; 2½% of the final A Level mark)

AO5i show understanding of the contexts in which literary texts are written and understood
(5% of the final AS mark; 2½% of the final A Level mark)

Content

This module meets the prose requirement for the syllabus. There is a choice of either pre-1900 or modern writing; there is also a choice of types of prose: the novel or the short story form.

Understanding your text

When you were very young you began to gain knowledge of stories. Take the tale of the Three Little Pigs. You will have known all about the three houses made of straw, wood and brick, and how the wolf huffed and puffed and blew down the first two. However, what did the fable mean? Only when you were older did you realise that this is a moral fable about the virtues of prudence, caution and wisdom.

And that's the difference between knowing and understanding; you knew the plot first, and then learned to understand themes. The word 'theme' is generally used to indicate the purposes or concerns of the writer – the deeper ideas that lie behind the plot.

ACTIVITY 1

In groups, remind yourselves of the tale of Little Red Riding Hood. First of all, work through the story, and then discuss what you think are the ideas or themes behind the plot.

When discussing the ideas behind the story you should ask yourself two questions:

- What ideas does the story convey to its readers or listeners?

- What lessons may be learned from the experiences of Little Red Riding Hood?

ACTIVITY 2

Now remind yourself of a novel or short story you read for GCSE. Draw two columns with the headings 'Plot' and 'Themes', then in your groups fill in the details under each heading.

Understanding the difference between plot and themes is the first stage of grasping the ideas of knowledge and understanding – the first part of the second Assessment Objective.

Now it is time to turn to more advanced work. First read the following extract, a paragraph from Chapter 7 of George Orwell's *Animal Farm*. The animals have rebelled, apparently successfully, against the cruel farmer, Jones. But their hopes are dashed because Napoleon and Squealer, two brutal pigs, are becoming just as tyrannical as the farmer.

Nevertheless, towards the end of January it became obvious that it would be necessary to procure some more grain from somewhere. In these days Napoleon rarely appeared in public, but spent all his time in the farmhouse, which was guarded at each door by fierce-looking dogs. When he did emerge it was in a ceremonial manner, with an escort of six dogs who closely surrounded him and growled if anyone came too near. Frequently he did not even appear on Sunday mornings, but issued his orders through one of the other pigs, usually Squealer.

First consider what is going on in the story or plot:

- the animals are short of food

- Napoleon keeps himself to himself

- he has guard dogs

- he has a second-in-command called Squealer who issues his orders.

Now consider the ideas that lie behind the story:

- things are tough for the starving animals

- Napoleon has changed – 'In these days . . .'

- he can terrorise the animals with his dogs

- he has taken on royal airs – his 'ceremonial manner'

- he is the general, with Squealer as one of his deputies.

In this example there is a sense of Napoleon's increasing power, of the poor situation of some of the other animals. This prepares the reader for the criticism of tyrannical dictatorship which is one of the main themes of this novel. This is a lot to glean from one short extract, and shows how closely you must learn to read and analyse your text to draw out the writer's ideas.

Here is an extract from E. M. Forster's *A Room with a View*. The heroine, Lucy, has agreed to marry Cecil, a young man with a snobbish attitude. Lucy lives with her noisy and happy family – her mother and her brother Freddy – in 'Windy Corner', an unspoilt and old-fashioned country house.

'Look out!' cried Freddy.

The curtains parted.

Cecil's first movement was one of irritation. He couldn't bear the Honeychurch habit of sitting in the dark to save the furniture. Instinctively he gave the curtains a twitch, and sent them swinging down their poles. Light entered. There was revealed a terrace, such as is owned by many villas, with trees each side of it, and on it a little rustic seat, and two flower-beds. But it was transfigured by the view beyond, for Windy Corner was built on the range that overlooks the Sussex Weald. Lucy, who was in the little seat, seemed on the edge of a green magic carpet which hovered in the air above the tremulous world.

ACTIVITY 3

Read the extract and use the model from Activity 2 to analyse it for yourself. First identify the plot and then the ideas behind the extract.

You are now well on the way towards achieving knowledge and understanding of a writer's ideas, which is the first part of the second Assessment Objective. However, this knowledge and understanding needs to involve consideration of the ways in which writers present their ideas. It is therefore time to turn to the third Assessment Objective, to 'show detailed understanding of the ways in which writers' choices of form, structure and language shape meanings'.

How writers shape meanings

It has sometimes been suggested that one of the differences between prose and poetry lies in the language used, that prose writers use 'everyday language'. This is a myth. To see why, let's analyse some of the ways in which words are used in poetry and in prose.

Writers of prose, like writers of poetry, use **figurative language** to bring words to life, to give them emphasis and impact, and to give words an extended range of meaning, as you will see in the next section.

Exploring the language of prose

In Alice Walker's novel, *The Color Purple*, the American female narrator has had a rotten childhood and and an equally rotten marriage. However, she has made a friendship with another woman who has taught her that there is beauty and love in life:

Naw, she say. God made it. Listen, God love everything you love – and a mess of stuff you don't. But more than anything else, God love admiration.

You saying God vain? I ast.

Naw, she say. Not vain, just wanting to share a good thing. I think it pisses God off if you walk by the color purple in a field somewhere and don't notice it.

In this extract the colour purple is used to indicate God's love, admiration and wonder. But the word 'purple' may also have other significances, such as:

- death and mourning

- the robes of royalty

- other significances personal to you.

So you have seen that the word 'purple' has gathered up many meanings. When these various meanings are generally agreed they are called **connotations** but when they are personal to the reader they are called **associations**.

ACTIVITY 4

Choose another colour such as red, black, white or gold, and list the different connotations and associations which occur to you.

Many words work in this way. Take the word 'woods'. The next extract is from Robert Frost's poem 'Stopping by Woods on a Snowy Evening':

> The woods are lovely, dark, and deep,
> But I have promises to keep,
> And miles to go before I sleep,
> And miles to go before I sleep.

Here the speaker cannot stop. What does the word 'woods' suggest? Could it be leisure time? Something that is secret and exciting? Or could it be death and peace?

The accumulation of a number of meanings around words also occurs in prose writing. Here is an extract from the novel *Hard Times* by Charles Dickens, in which an unpleasant character called Mrs Sparsit is eavesdropping in the hope of bringing trouble to a young girl:

> She thought of the wood, and stole towards it, heedless of long grass and briars: of worms, snails, and slugs, and all the creeping things that be. With her dark eyes and her hook nose warily in advance of her, Mrs. Sparsit softly crushed her way through the thick undergrowth, so intent upon her object that she would probably have done no less, if the wood had been a wood of adders.

Here the word 'wood' has a different set of connotations linked to unpleasant creatures like snails, and slugs and adders. Woods are a place of danger, and with Mrs Sparsit included, possibly evil. To make sure that you realise this, Dickens repeats the word 'wood' three times.

Remember too that 'woods' has many connotations for you from your childhood memories and earlier reading. For example, Little Red Riding Hood met the wolf in the woods, and Hansel and Gretel nearly died there. Shakespeare, as in *A Midsummer Night's Dream*, uses woods to suggest an area of magic, dreams, love and secrecy.

ACTIVITY 5

Choose a couple of words such as 'sea', 'snow', 'fire' or 'water'. Write down the connotations and associations that these words hold for you. It may be interesting to compare these with a partner's.

Prose writers don't simply choose individual words carefully; like the writers of poetry, they use imagery to draw attention to what they are writing about, and to try to make the reader see things in a new or unusual light. Imagery allows writers to suggest links or comparisons between one idea or object and another, to achieve particular effects. Sometimes the link is unsurprising, but equally it can be unexpected or even shocking, adding power and impact to the words and ideas. This makes the reader use his or her imagination and experience to form an impression of what the writer is trying to convey.

You will no doubt remember these from your GCSE studies, but it is wise to remind yourself about **similes** and **metaphors**.

Similes

Think of how you might describe a child or a friend. You could say 'She is as pretty as a picture' or 'He is as sweet as sugar', or that a boxer 'fought like a lion'. Each of these examples uses a simile, a comparison of two things linked by the words 'as' or 'like'. How do these comparisons work?

'She is as pretty as a picture' calls up a visual image. She is compared to a beautiful painting, so the image reinforces the idea of perfection. That is the point of this simile.

'He is as sweet as sugar' works in a different and slightly more complicated way. This time the words suggest taste, the sweetness of sugar; the boy is sweet, but perhaps sugar can be too sweet? The second possibility conveys the suggestion that the sweetness could be a little too much, a little overdone.

Finally here, 'He fought like a lion' is yet more complicated. The qualities that we link to a lion, and therefore to the man, could be strength, power, danger, wildness, courage, fear. There is also a sense of touch here, implied in the thought of those dreadful claws tearing at somebody or something.

ACTIVITY 6

Write six sentences that use similes with the words 'as' and 'like'; try to incorporate the different senses of taste, touch, sight, sound and smell. Following the model above, try to explain the effects of the similes you created.

How do similes appear in literary texts? You probably commented upon the use of similes at GCSE. Here is an example of the use of simile in poetry. This is an extract from Wilfred Owen's poem 'Dulce et Decorum Est', in which he writes about the experiences of soldiers in the First World War. He describes the face of a dying man, the victim of a gas attack, who is being thrown onto the collection wagon:

If in smothering dreams you too could pace
Behind the wagon that we flung him in,
And watch the white eyes writhing in his face,
His hanging face, like a devil's sick of sin; [. . .]

The last simile is startling: 'like a devil's [face] sick of sin'. How does it work? Brave soldiers are not normally linked with the devil, so the image shocks. This may suggest that the things usually associated with a man have disappeared, probably because of war. The face is not any devil's face, but the face of a devil who has experienced so much evil, so much hell, that even he is sick of it. The word 'devil' makes us think of Hell and therefore of evil deeds, so perhaps war is Hell?

ACTIVITY 7

These are the first two lines of the poem 'Dulce et Decorum Est':

> Bent double, like old beggars under sacks,
> Knock-kneed, coughing like hags, we cursed through sludge, [. . .]

There are two similes here. Working alone or in groups, analyse the ways in which these similes work.

The use of similes is also important in prose writing. Here is an extract from *The Virgin and the Gypsy* by D. H. Lawrence. In this novel a young, innocent and inexperienced girl has fallen in love for the first time. She has her first sexual feelings – for a gypsy, a forbidden love for a girl of her social class.

At length he put down his coffee-cup by the fire, then looked round at her. Her hair fell across her face as she tried to sip from the hot cup. On her face was that tender look of sleep, which a nodding flower has when it is full out. Like a mysterious early flower, she was full out, like a snowdrop which spreads its three white wings in a flight into the waking sleep of its brief blossoming. The waking sleep of her full-opened virginity, entranced like a snowdrop in the sunshine, was upon her.

Two of Lawrence's similes are: 'Like a mysterious early flower' and 'like a snowdrop which spreads its three white wings'. The first of these, 'like a mysterious early flower', tells us about the girl:

- there is some shyness, something unknown or unexplored about the girl

- she has the beauty of a flower

- she has the delicacy of a flower.

But the simile also introduces a threat, the flower is 'early'. This reflects the idea that the girl is young, rather fragile. Think about what happens to early flowers – they also *die* early, don't they? What is going to die or disappear?

ACTIVITY 8

The second simile is: 'like a snowdrop which spreads its three white wings'. What impressions do you receive from this image? You should include in your ideas the particular qualities of a snowdrop and how they could relate to the girl, the significance of the words 'wings' and 'white', and Lawrence's use of the terms 'waking sleep', 'brief' and 'blossoming'.

You will have realised that all the words work together to make us ask questions about what Lawrence wants us to see, or to think about the girl. These thoughts and questions help to create many meanings, and to gather meanings as we read on. This is called a **cumulative process**.

ACTIVITY 9

Lawrence uses a third simile: 'like a snowdrop in the sunshine'. Working alone or in a group, analyse the ways in which the simile is effective.

Metaphors

A metaphor works like a condensed and abbreviated simile, without the words 'as' or 'like'. It is a form of comparison in which one thing is given the qualities of another. For example, if you say 'Eric stretched himself to the limit in his studies', you don't mean that he literally stretched himself; the image is of forcibly extending something – a piece of elastic, say – to suggest how hard the boy worked. As in poetry, the use of metaphor is important to writers of prose texts.

In your everyday speech you often use metaphors. If you were to describe someone as a 'wet blanket', you would mean that that person has reduced or 'dampened' your enjoyment just as a wet blanket may be used to put out a fire.

ACTIVITY 10

Make a list of six examples of your use of metaphor in everyday speech.

Metaphors are in many ways the 'building blocks' of both prose and poetry writing. Writers use metaphors to create layers of meaning in their poetry. Here is the first line of Andrew Young's poem 'Hard Frost', in which the frost of winter is seen to battle against Nature before being defeated by the sun:

Frost called to water 'Halt!'

ACTIVITY 11

What sort of metaphor is being used here? What effects do you think that Young achieves through this use?

Here is the final verse of 'Hard Frost':

But vainly the fierce frost
Interns poor fish, ranks trees in an armed host,
Hangs daggers from house-eaves
And on the windows ferny ambush weaves;
In the long war grown warmer
The sun will strike him dead and strip his armour.

The whole **stanza** is an extended metaphor in which frost is seen as an aggressive soldier. The idea works by grabbing your attention: it creates links between two things that are essentially unlike each other, frost and a soldier. The military metaphor is sustained throughout the verse with the use of the language of war such as 'Interns', 'hangs daggers', 'ambush weaves'; and the sun, finally the victor, 'will strike him dead and strip his armour'. Andrew Young tries to put a new spin on our idea of Winter. The metaphor works through the use of a military **register**.

The use of metaphors is often just as important to writers of prose as it is to writers of poetry. Here is an extract from Tom Wolfe's novel *The Bonfire of the Vanities*, in which he criticises the greed, materialism and consumerism of twentieth-century American life. Here the central character, Sherman McCoy, has just arrived at a society party and is surveying the women he sees there:

The women came in two varieties. First, there were women in their late thirties and in their forties and older (women of 'a certain age'), all of them skin and bones (starved to near perfection) [. . .] They were the social X-rays, to use the phrase that had bubbled up into Sherman's own brain. Second there were the so-called Lemon Tarts. These were women in their twenties or early thirties, mostly blondes (the Lemon in the Tarts), who were the second, third, or fourth wives or live-in girlfriends of men over forty or fifty or sixty (or seventy), the sort of women men refer to, quite without thinking, as *girls*. [. . .] What was entirely missing from *chez* Bavardage was that manner of woman who is neither very young nor very old, who has laid in a lining of subcutaneous fat, who glows with plumpness and a rosy face that speaks, without a word, of home and earth [. . .] and conversations while seated on the edge of the bed, just before the Sandman comes. In short, no one ever invited . . . Mother.

This single paragraph makes a cutting attack on the nature of society life in modern New York. The effect rests on a sequence of seven metaphors, but Tom Wolfe uses these metaphors in a very clever way by using two contrasted sets of images.

He uses the first two metaphors to show up what he actually sees in this society he ridicules:

- The 'social X-rays': these are the fashionable anorexic socialites. The force of the metaphor is that these women are so thin that you could see through them as if they were X-ray films, because it was considered to be socially desirable.

- The 'Lemon Tarts': these are the typical hangers-on to rich men whom he sees in his society. To avoid a lengthy account of their appearance the author gives us the reason why he uses this expression.

These first two metaphors, therefore, describe the women whom McCoy sees as he looks around the room. To complete this criticism, the author then goes on to explain what is missing in this society in the next sequence of five metaphors:

- The woman 'who has laid in a lining of subcutaneous fat': this is an image of a normal woman of average build. She obviously has not consciously gathered her subcutaneous fat, but the verb is used to suggest that she is not so fashion-conscious that she will stop eating well enough to line herself with a layer of fat.

- She 'glows with plumpness and a rosy face': the metaphorical word 'glows' suggests that such a woman has a healthy bloom to her skin and rosy cheeks, unlike the pallid 'X-rays'.

- She 'speaks, without a word, of home and earth': this sort of woman represents a value quite different from the first two types. She does not literally 'speak', as the author explains in case you miss the point, but she suggests the value of quiet home life and natural, earthy things.

- '. . . before the Sandman comes': here Wolfe offers a metaphor suggesting an image of secure family life. The Sandman represents sleep; this is the sort of language you would use to a child who is drifting off to sleep. But children are not seen in the society Wolfe criticises here.

- 'In short, no one ever invited . . . Mother'; this last sentence is very important in the sequence.

The word 'mother' is important because the author has spent the whole paragraph building up to this. Mothers are the key to society and social well-being – they have the children and hold families together, and therefore should lie at the heart of society. But in this society, which Wolfe sees as artificial, mothers are not welcome. The metaphor lies in the word 'mother', as Wolfe is connoting here not just mothers in the literal sense, but those women who hold family-based values and who don't fit in with the company of the trendy New Yorkers of the novel.

Tom Wolfe uses metaphor as a type of shorthand to attack his society while expending very few words, and achieves his desired effect.

There are two other matters of style for you to consider here: word order, and pacing. Writers pick their word-order carefully, and important words usually occur at the beginning or end of sentences. Here the key word 'Mother' is held until the very last word of the paragraph. As for pacing, note how Tom Wolfe has paced the important last line of this extract: he puts in three dots to create a deliberate pause before the important last word. This has the effect of making the reader briefly wonder what to expect.

The whole paragraph is carefully controlled through choice of language, word-order and pacing.

ACTIVITY 12

Carefully write out the passage above in plain English, without using any figurative language at all. You'll almost certainly find that your rewritten passage is much longer than the original. This should show you how figurative language is used by prose writers as a shorthand, to achieve good effects with great economy.

For your final exercise in this section on figurative language, read this extract from the novel *One Flew Over the Cuckoo's Nest* by Ken Kesey, which is about inmates in an asylum. Kesey sees the inmates as victims of society, which he calls the Combine, and sarcastically presents the hospital as a mending factory for society, run by Big Nurse. The narrator is an inmate:

Yes. This is what I know. The ward is a factory for the Combine. It's for fixing up mistakes made in the neighbourhoods and in the schools and in the churches, the hospital is. When a completed product goes back out into society, all fixed up as good as new, *better* than new sometimes, it brings joy to the Big Nurse's heart; something that came in all twisted different is now a functioning, adjusted component, a credit to the whole outfit and a marvel to behold. Watch him sliding across the land with a welded grin, fitting into some nice little neighbourhood where they're just now digging trenches along the street to lay pipes for city water. He's happy with it. He's adjusted to surroundings finally . . .

ACTIVITY 13

Using the model above, working alone or in groups, analyse the sequence of metaphors. Then explore how they are effective in achieving what you think the author's purposes are.

You will have realised from these considerations of the language of prose that it bears many similarities to the language of poetry. You need to scrutinise the language of your novel or short story as closely as you will look at the language of your poetry when you move on to Module 2.

You are also building up a critical vocabulary, which will help you to gain marks in achieving the 'appropriate terminology' of the first Assessment Objective. So far, you have considered connotation, association, cumulative effect, similes, metaphors, word-order and pacing. But:

> Warning: you must remember that these terms are meaningless in themselves. They only have life when used as a shorthand to explain how writers achieve their meaning. Critical terms identified in isolation from expression of meaning have no value. You should always try to explain how figures of speech are used to achieve particular effects.

Now the two questions you asked about prose in Activity 1 have become three:

- What ideas is the writer trying to convey to readers?

- What experience or experiences is the writer trying to convey?

- How is the writer trying to convey these ideas?

However, language is used in other, more specific ways in the writing of novels and short stories. You must broaden your perspectives in order to complete your work on the third Assessment Objective. First you will look at varieties of prose writing, then move on to consider structure and structural devices.

Varieties of prose writing

Narrative prose

All the prose you read for this module, whether in novel or short story form, is narrative prose in that it narrates or tells a story. But this broad description is not enough to define the full range of prose you will encounter. There are several types of prose writing, and you may well find that your own text includes several types.

Look at the beginning of *The Secret Agent*, a novel by Joseph Conrad:

> Mr. Verloc, going out in the morning, left his shop nominally in charge of his brother-in-law. It could be done, because there was very little business at any time, and practically none at all before the evening. Mr. Verloc cared but little about his ostensible business. And, moreover, his wife was in charge of his brother-in-law.
>
> The shop was small, and so was the house [. . .] In the daytime the door remained closed; in the evening it stood discreetly but suspiciously ajar.

On a first reading it seems that just a few facts are given: Mr Verloc has a shop that is not particularly busy, so he is free to go out in the daytime and leave his wife to run the business. You also learn that for some reason she has to look after her brother. That is the narrative or storytelling element of the opening chapter.

But if you look at the words carefully, you see that there is something else going on, and begin to ask a few questions:

- If there is so little business, why does Verloc keep the shop open?

- Where does Verloc go in the day when he leaves his business?

- Isn't it odd that all the business is done in the evening?

- Why does Conrad write that in the evening the door was 'suspiciously ajar'?

This sequence of ideas puts queries into the readers' minds; and indeed the shop turns out to be the centre of terrorist activities.

ACTIVITY 14

Look at the first two paragraphs of the set text you are studying. How does the writer prepare readers for what is to come?

Prose used emotively

An author may use language to move the reader or to draw out a sympathetic response, as well as to inform the reader. Dickens is a master of this technique. Rachael is the heroine of *Hard Times*. In this extract she is taking care of a character called Stephen, who is distressed and disturbed:

> He had a violent fit of trembling, and then sunk into his chair. After a time he controlled himself, and, resting with an elbow on one knee, and his head upon that hand, could look towards Rachael. Seen across the dim candle with his moistened eyes, she looked as if she had a glory shining round her head. He could have believed that she had. He did believe it, . . .

How does Dickens create an emotional, or possibly sentimental, effect in this extract? Stephen, sunk into a chair, is gazing up at Rachael in an attitude you could think of as adoration, his 'moistened eyes' creating a sentimental image of tearful gratitude. The light is dim, and Rachael is seen as having a halo around her head; she is presented as a sort of angel. Using the trick of repetition with the words 'believed' and 'believe', Dickens forces the reader to see Rachael as Stephen sees her.

Thomas Hardy also uses emotive language to secure an emotional response from his readers. In his novel *Tess of the d'Urbervilles*, the innocent Tess is the central character and endures a life of suffering. Running away from society she takes refuge in a wood, where she hears strange noises:

Then she perceived what had been going on to disturb her [. . .] Under the trees several pheasants lay about, their rich plumage dabbled with blood; some were dead, some feebly twitching a wing, some staring up at the sky, some pulsating quickly, some contorted, some stretched out – all of them writhing in agony, except the fortunate ones whose tortures had ended during the night by the inability of nature to bear more.

Tess decides to end their misery:

'Poor darlings – to suppose myself the most miserable being on earth in the sight o' such misery as yours!' she exclaimed, her tears running down as she killed the birds tenderly . . .

ACTIVITY 15

Analyse the ways in which Hardy creates an emotional scene here. You need to look at the verbs and adverbs. And you must consider the **dialogue**: why does Hardy put these words into Tess's mouth? What effect does this achieve?

Subjective prose

In **subjective** prose, the writer carefully creates a picture and meaning to try to make the reader respond in a certain way. D. H. Lawrence writes likes this in his novel *Sons and Lovers* when he describes the sort of house that Mrs Morel, a miner's wife, lives in:

The houses themselves were substantial and very decent. One could walk all round, seeing little front gardens with auriculas and saxifrage in the shadow of the bottom block, sweet-williams and pinks in the sunny top block; seeing neat front windows, little porches, little privet hedges, and dormer windows for the attics. But that was outside; that was the view on to the uninhabited parlours of all the colliers' wives. The dwelling-room, the kitchen, was at the back of the house, facing inward between the blocks, looking at a scrubby back garden, and then at the ash-pits. And between the rows, between the long lines of ash-pits, went the alley, where the children played and the women gossiped and the men smoked. So the actual conditions of living in the Bottoms, that was so well-built and that looked so nice, were quite unsavoury because people must live in the kitchen, and the kitchens opened on to that nasty alley of ash-pits.

Lawrence quite clearly manipulates the reader's response to these houses; he is determined that the viewpoint which he himself holds is accepted.

ACTIVITY 16

Analyse the ways in which Lawrence secures the response that he intends the reader to have. Look at the way in which the passage breaks into two sections with the word 'but'. Analyse the positive nouns and adjectives in the first part of the passage, and the ways in which Lawrence reverses the mood and tone through negative language in the second part of the passage.

Lyrical prose

Lyrical prose is often used to establish a positive atmosphere in literature. It is prose that is poetic in its force, using the sorts of devices introduced earlier in this section. In this extract from *Things Fall Apart*, Chinua Achebe offers us a picture of life in an African village; a young boy, Nwoye, is growing up and has to spend more time with his father, Okonkwo, than with his mother:

So Okonkwo encouraged the boys to sit with him in his *obi* [large living quarters of the head of the family], and he told them stories of the land – masculine stories of violence and bloodshed. Nwoye knew that it was right to be masculine and to be violent, but somehow he preferred the stories that his mother used to tell, and which she no doubt still told to her younger children – stories of the tortoise and his wily ways, and of the bird *eneke-nti-oba* who challenged the whole world to a wrestling contest and was finally thrown by the cat.

What is Achebe doing in this passage? You realise that the boy has passed from childhood to youth; he has to leave the innocent folk tales of his mother and listen to the warlike stories of his father. You feel sympathy for the young boy: he is almost unwilling to grow up, and would still prefer to be with his mother. Achebe briefly describes two of the village myths, giving a sense of the innocence and simplicity of traditional African village life that is about to be wrecked by the arrival of the missionaries with their more modern beliefs. A whole culture is about to disappear.

F. Scott Fitzgerald is acclaimed for the lyrical, poetic quality of his prose writing. In his novel *The Great Gatsby*, Fitzgerald describes the elegant life of the rich, which Gatsby has disastrously aimed to achieve. Here is a description of the house of one wealthy couple:

We walked through a high hallway into a bright rosy-coloured space, fragilely bound into the house by french windows at either end. The windows were ajar and gleaming white against the fresh grass outside that seemed to grow a little way into the house. A breeze blew through the room, blew curtains in at one end and out the other like pale flags, twisting them up toward the frosted wedding-cake of the ceiling, and then rippled over the wine-coloured rug, making a shadow on it as wind does on the sea.

Here Fitzgerald creates a real feeling of wealth and comfort, and of things somehow being right.

ACTIVITY 17

Earlier in this chapter you looked at figurative language used in prose. Using the knowledge that you have now gained, analyse the ways in which Fitzgerald uses this sort of poetic language to achieve effect in the passage.

Gothic prose

You will be familiar from your experience of cinema and video with the idea of the Gothic. This type of prose has certain characteristics. There may be ideas of the supernatural; of haunted castles; of ghosts or vampires; of the peculiar servant; of storms and thunder and lightning; of an innocent character exposed to shock-horrors. This style occurs in the writing of Mary Shelley and Ann Bronte, and to some extent in Charlotte Bronte's *Jane Eyre*. Here is an extract from one of the most famous Gothic short stories, *The Fall of the House of Usher* by Edgar Allan Poe. In this extract, the narrator has his first sight of the house and its surroundings, and is fearful of what he sees:

I looked upon the scene before me – upon the mere house, and the simple landscape features of the domain – upon the bleak walls – upon the vacant eye-like windows – upon a few rank sedges – and upon a few white trunks of decayed trees – with an utter depression of soul which I can compare to no earthly sensation more properly than to the after-dream of the reveller upon opium – the bitter lapse into every-day life – the hideous dropping off of the veil. There was an iciness, a sinking, a sickening of the heart [. . .] I reined horse to the precipitous brink of a black and lurid tarn [a small mountain lake] that lay in unruffled lustre by the dwelling, and gazed down – but with a shudder even more thrilling than before – upon the remodelled and inverted images of the grey sedge [a marsh grass], and the ghastly tree-stems, and vacant and eye-like windows.

ACTIVITY 18

Working in groups, analyse the ways in which the writer creates the Gothic sense of fear and of anxiety. Include in your analysis: the punctuation, including the effects of the dashes; the use of verbs, adverbs and adjectives; the use of the senses; and the use of colour.

Satirical prose

In satirical prose the writer aims to attack society by ridiculing problems within it. You may well have read or seen the television adaptation of *Pride and Prejudice*. In the novel Jane Austen, one of the great satirists, criticises society's attitude towards love and marriage amongst other things. She declares her intention at the very beginning of the novel by mocking the attitudes of people in the neighbourhood when a wealthy young man joins their circle:

It is a truth universally acknowledged, that a single man in possession of a good fortune, must be in want of a wife.

However little known the feelings or views of such a man may be on his first entering the neighbourhood, this truth is so well fixed in the minds of the surrounding families, that he is considered the rightful property of some one or other of their daughters.

The humour here, and the **satire,** lies in the mockery of the materialistic hopes of the neighbourhood. It is these people who hold the 'truth universally acknowledged', a truth of which the young man himself is obviously unaware. He has no idea that so many ambitions are being centred on him.

Austen achieves the effect because her style is tongue-in-cheek and ironic. She uses a lot of dialogue so that characters condemn themselves out of their own mouths. Perhaps the funniest example of this may be the scene in *Pride and Prejudice* where Mr Collins proposes to Elizabeth Bennet. Jane Austen makes it clear to the reader what a fool Mr Collins is. He concludes his ill-judged proposal in this way:

'And now nothing remains for me but to assure you in the most animated language of the violence of my affection. To fortune I am perfectly indifferent, and shall make no demand of that nature on your father, since I am well aware that it could not be complied with; [. . .] On that head, therefore, I shall be uniformly silent; and you may assure yourself that no ungenerous reproach shall ever pass my lips when we are married.'

ACTIVITY 19

Look carefully at the language and the ideas of the passage about Mr Collins's proposal. What do you learn about Mr Collins himself, and about his attitudes towards marriage and towards Elizabeth Bennet?

This technique is also employed by modern writers such as Alison Lurie. In her novel *The Last Resort*, Lurie satirises or mocks the behaviour of the residents of Key West, a Florida Key, and visiting tourists. She focuses on the vanity, greed and pretension of the residents, and the wide-eyed naivety of the tourists. In this extract Molly, one of the residents, is complaining about the tourist train that allows visitors to gawp at what they see from its windows:

'She was very eager to go,' said Molly, who had never been on the train, though it passed her house continually. The day she and her husband first moved in, the loudspeaker had called the tourists' attention to a large tropical tree with loose, flaky bark that grew in their side yard. 'On your left, just ahead, you will see a fine specimen of one of Key West's native trees. It is a gumbo limbo, but natives call it the tourist tree, because it is always red and peeling.'

The first time Molly and her husband heard this joke they laughed [But they tire of the joke and try to get the commentary stopped] [. . .] Polite calls to the Conch Train office [the conch is a shellfish that Key West's first residents fished and ate] over the next few weeks accomplished nothing; the woman who answered the phone appeared to think that Molly should feel honored to have her tree noticed.

ACTIVITY 20

Analyse this extract and pick out the attitudes being satirised. You might include: the attitude of Molly and her husband; the guide's attitude towards the tourists, including the commentary dialogue and what it implies about the visiting tourists; and the attitude of the lady from the Conch Train office.

The use of prose with factual language

In his novel *Down and Out in Paris and London*, George Orwell sets out to present the wretched conditions of poor low-level restaurant workers in Paris and tramps in London. In the first part of the book he relies on the use of vivid detail to engage the reader. In this extract the narrator sees the place where he will live:

My hotel was called the Hôtel des Trois Moineaux. It was a dark, rickety warren of five storeys, cut up by wooden partitions into forty rooms. The rooms were small and inveterately dirty, for there was no maid, and Madame F., the *patronne*, had no time to do any sweeping. The walls were as thin as matchwood, and to hide the cracks they had been covered with layer after layer of pink paper, which had come loose and housed innumerable bugs.

Notice that Orwell states facts in order to emphasise the poor living conditions; he makes very little use of figurative language. He presents a clear picture of the hotel, and lets the facts speak for themselves. Later he employs another sort of language when he discusses London's tramps:

The following figures, published by the LCC from a night census taken on February 13th, 1931, will show the relative numbers of destitute men and destitute women:

Spending the night in the streets, 60 men, 18 women.
In shelters and homes not licensed as common lodging houses, 1,057 men, 137 women. [. . .]

Here Orwell provides the reader with numerical details offering precise and accurate information. Why do you think that he varies his style like this? Here are some possible reasons:

- The variety of prose style keeps the reader interested.

- Orwell allows the clear descriptions of the living conditions to create a quite shocking picture in the reader's mind.

- The change from factual description to official information gives us a sense that the author knows what he is talking about.

- These numerical details give the text the appearance of an authoritative document.

Mixing prose styles

You may want to consider why Orwell deliberately mixes prose styles in this way. The technique is also used by contemporary writers. Here is Sebastian Faulks, in his novel *Birdsong*, writing about the horrors of the First World War. Unusually, he is writing about the dangers facing tunnellers (the men who laid mines, often directly beneath enemy positions), and employs a similar mix of language and style to that used by Orwell. At times, Faulks offers a factual account of the work of those who dig the tunnels:

Jack Firebrace lay forty-five feet underground with several hundred thousand tons of France above his face. He could hear the wooden wheezing of the feed that pumped air through the tunnel. Most of it was exhausted by the time it reached him. His back was supported by a wooden cross, his feet against the clay, facing towards the enemy. With an adapted spade, he loosened quantities of soil into a bag which he passed back to Evans, his mate, who then crawled away in the darkness.

The style here seems to be **detached** or **objective**, with the author conveying facts rather than emotions. Faulks gives clear details of the depth at which the men work, and of the dangerous nature of the tunnellers' work, and chooses to let the facts speak for themselves. Elsewhere the style changes when Faulks tries to draw an engaged, emotional response from his readers. An example of this is the incident when a recovery party goes in search of men killed in an underground explosion. They find the bodies:

Bright and sleek on liver, a rat emerged from the abdomen; it levered and flopped fatly over the ribs, glutted with pleasure. Bit by bit on to stretchers, what flesh fell left in mud. Not men, but flies and flesh, thought Stephen. Brennan anxiously stripping a torso with no head. He clasped it with both hands, dragged legless up from the crater, his fingers vanishing into buttered green flesh. It was his brother.

ACTIVITY 21

Working in groups, analyse the ways in which the language works to express meaning in the first *Birdsong* extract, then repeat this exercise for the second extract. Compare the differences in the language used in each case, and discuss what effects the author achieves by varying his prose style.

Impressionistic prose styles

Impressionistic writing styles were important in the development of the twentieth-century novel. The two authors who spring to mind are Virginia Woolf and James Joyce. This extract from the beginning of Woolf's *Mrs Dalloway* shows how the approach works:

Mrs Dalloway said she would buy the flowers herself.

For Lucy [Mrs Dalloway's maid] had her work cut out for her. The doors would be taken off their hinges; Rumpelmayer's men [hired to set up the party] were coming. And then, thought Clarissa Dalloway, what a morning – fresh as if issued to children on a beach.

What a lark! What a plunge! For so it had always seemed to her when, with a little squeak of the hinges, which she could hear now, she had burst open the French windows and plunged at Bourton into the open air. How fresh, how calm, stiller than this of course, the air was in the early morning; like the flap of a wave; the kiss of a wave; [. . .]

This extract is a series of impressions from within the mind of Clarissa Dalloway. The facts are limited: she is going to have a party, preparations are already underway, and she has had parties like this before.

But how important are these facts? Are they the main point of the passage? Probably, the answer is no. What is original here is that we are given Mrs Dalloway's thoughts as she thinks them – a technique called **stream of consciousness**. How does it work?

You see that Mrs Dalloway enjoys life and is enthusiastic. You get to know her through her use of images of the beach and of the sea, key to her way of thinking, with the words 'fresh', and 'flap' and 'kiss' – all positive words of enjoyment and movement. The character's senses are used to convey the feelings more powerfully, and there is also a flashback to the past at Bourton. In other words, the prose has been written to convey the thoughts of the woman, as they occur, through a series of impressions. It is these thoughts that are important, giving the reader a glimpse into Mrs Dalloway's mind, rather than any narrative development of plot.

ACTIVITY 22

Write out the extract in a traditional narrative sequence to explore how Mrs Dalloway moves from the present to the past in her thoughts. Try to work out the key images that she uses, and consider their effects.

Prose of psychological analysis

The final type of writing to be considered also goes inwards, into the mind of the character. Like impressionistic writing, this is one of the main developments of twentieth-century prose. In this extract from *The Sea, The Sea* by Iris Murdoch the central character, Charles Arrowby, narrates his own story and frequently pauses in the narrative account to share his thoughts with the reader. Here he has just re-met an old girlfriend whom he thinks he has treated badly:

I am moved by having seen Lizzie and am wondering whether I have been clever or foolish. Of course if I had taken poor Lizzie in my arms it would all have been over in a second. At the moment when she hurled her handbag away she was ready to give in, to make every concession, to utter every promise. And how much I wanted to seize her. This ghost embrace remains with me as a joy mislaid. (I must admit that, after having seen her, my ideas are a good deal less 'abstract'!) Yet perhaps it was wise, and I feel satisfied with my firmness.

There is a lot going on in this passage. The character addresses the reader directly, creating quite a close relationship as you feel you get to know him from the inside. Yet you still get a sense of the character of Charles – he is sure he could have seduced Lizzie, so is he a little bit arrogant? Look at his language – 'a joy mislaid'. Is he slightly stuffy or formal or old-fashioned?

The reader has already seen this episode a little earlier in the book; now it appears again, this time from another perspective. In fact, Iris Murdoch has created a style and approach that allows you to see people and situations from multiple perspectives; you gain a rounded view of them and are not forced to accept one viewpoint. In Murdoch's writing, as in Woolf's, you are given character studies of greater depth than in many other types of novel.

Here is an extract written as a traditional third-person narrative account from Michael Dibdin's novel *The Long Finish*, a detective story. The chief suspect, Minot, is about to be arrested for the second time on suspicion of murder:

That first time, the evening before, Minot had just finished eating a bowl of the lentil soup he made every Sunday, and which sat in its cauldron on the stove for the rest of the week. Eating lentils made you rich, his father had told him; every one you swallowed would come back one day as a gold coin. [. . .]

When he'd finished eating, Minot sluiced out the bowl under the tap and left it to dry. Then he went next door, sat down and turned on the television [. . .] He could only get two channels [. . .] but Minot didn't care. He wasn't interested in any of the programmes anyway. He just liked having the set on. It made the room more lively.

ACTIVITY 23

Rewrite this extract from the viewpoint of Minot in the style of either Virginia Woolf or Iris Murdoch, trying to use the sort of language that you think your chosen author would make her character use.

In this section you have considered various types of narrative prose writing: emotive, subjective, lyrical, Gothic, and satirical prose; prose involving the use of accurate, factual language; impressionistic prose writing; and prose of psychological analysis. In other words, you have now looked at form – the novel or short story – and types of writing within that form. You have explored the language of prose; so to complete the work required for AO3 it is time to consider structure and structural devices.

Structure and structural devices

Structure is not the same thing as narrative sequence, where you make a list of what happens in each successive part, chapter or section of the book. The word 'structure' means the ways in which the writer makes all the different elements of the book hang together or fuse into a whole work. To say this formally, structure and structural devices are the ways in which the writer imposes unity on his or her novel or short story.

Some of the most important ways of achieving this unity will emerge as you explore the following structural devices:

- appendices

- epilogue

- continuous narrative

- dialogue

- the use of viewpoint:
  - first- and third-person narration
  - the viewpoint of a child
  - the use of letters

- split narrative

- interior monologue

- character

- setting

- repetition and repetitive motifs

- flashback

- time shifts.

Appendices

Sometimes at the end of the narrative sequence of a novel, when the plot has run its course, the writer may add an appendix or appendices. Normally the word refers to sections added to the end of a book, but some writers use appendices to create a particular effect on the structure and therefore the possible meanings of a book.

For example, Ian McEwan attaches two appendices at the end of *Enduring Love*. In the main section of this novel the reader is offered an account of a love which is enduring in a horrific sense: an obsessive love that the character Jed has developed in a most threatening way for the central character, Joe. You come to realise that Jed is mentally sick. The first appendix is a case history of patients suffering from a similar problem, de Clérambault's syndrome. The second appendix is a final letter from Jed to Joe.

You must ask yourself why McEwan adds these appendices. There are several possible reasons for including the first appendix. For example, the account of patients suffering from this illness may modify your response to the character Jed, so you can now look back over the narrative and see things in a different light. Perhaps the whole novel changes its nature somewhat and takes on the form of a case history; this in turn may affect your response to the evidently mad Jed, by making you feel sympathy for him.

There is also a shift in the type of language used, as was discussed earlier in the writing of Orwell and Faulks. The medical register may persuade you that the author knows what he is talking about. The shift helps to create variety for the reader.

In the second appendix McEwan presents a final letter. The reader is given some background information:

Letter collected from Mr J. Parry, written towards end of his third year after admittance. Original filed with patient's notes. [. . .]

The letter concludes:

Thank you for loving me, thank you for accepting me, thank you for recognising what I am doing for our love. Send me a new message soon, and remember – faith is joy.

Jed

ACTIVITY 24

What are the effects of this final letter? How do you respond to Jed now? Does this affect your sympathies? How do you respond to Joe now? Do you think he may have contacted Jed? What do you think the future holds for Joe in his relationship with Jed?

Does McEwan achieve a double-take here? Are your sympathies shifted back to Joe with the future problems he will face from Jed? The events are ongoing, so do you agree that in this way the events of the novel are projected beyond the actual end of the novel?

Epilogue

Sometimes this effect is achieved by the use of an **epilogue**, often in the form of a direct address to the reader by the author. Here is an example from Jane Austen's novel *Mansfield Park*. The central character, Fanny Price, is an exemplary heroine full of virtues, in contrast to those around her. After many trials and tribulations, she is rewarded for her goodness and achieves recognition of her worth and a happy marriage. Although Jane Austen does not describe it as such, Chapter 48 acts as an epilogue. This extract comes from the beginning of the chapter:

Let other pens dwell on guilt and misery. I quit such odious subjects as soon as I can, impatient to restore everybody, not greatly in fault themselves, to tolerable comfort, and to have done with all the rest.

My Fanny indeed at this very time, I have the satisfaction of knowing, must have been happy in spite of every thing.

Then Austen goes on to describe the outcomes for the other characters after the conclusion of the novel.

ACTIVITY 25

Why has Jane Austen written in this way? Work in groups, and base your discussion on the following questions:

- Why does Jane Austen call Fanny Price 'My'?

- Why does Jane Austen choose to address the reader directly?

- What is Jane Austen's relationship with the reader now?

- Why does she choose to describe the events that happen after the course of the novel has been completed?

- What sort of tone and language is she employing here?

Continuous narrative

Continuous narrative is the traditional prose style of novels or short stories where events develop in a logical, chronological sequence. Here you may well see a character's life in an apparently realistic time sequence. Most of our nineteenth-century novelists write in this way, including Dickens, Hardy and Eliot. Some present writers also use this method. Jill Paton Walsh, in her novel *Knowledge of Angels*, uses this form of narrative to create a sense of the epic and important historical events that unfold as a youth arrives on an island, establishes a controversial religion, and dies a martyr:

Above the woods the mountain was almost sheer for thousands of feet, and they moved slowly on the narrow shelves that served for paths.

The style is detailed and apparently realistic. In her introduction to the book Jill Paton Walsh explains how the knowledge of the reader is like that of angels:

a hovering, gravely attentive presence, observing everything, from whom nothing is concealed, [. . .]

ACTIVITY 26

What do you think the author means here, and why do you think she uses continuous prose?

Dialogue

Dialogue is very important in most novels, and is of great use as a shorthand for the author to develop ideas.

Here is a short piece of dialogue from Sylvia Plath's novel *The Bell Jar*. The narrator is Esther, the central character; she has had a breakdown, partly because of a bad relationship with her mother and partly in response to her father's death. Esther has been to hospital for electric shock therapy but has decided to stop this; her mother comes to collect her:

'I'm through with that Doctor Gordon,' I said, after we had left Dodo and her black wagon behind the pines. 'You can call him up and tell him I'm not coming next week.'

My mother smiled. 'I knew my baby wasn't like that.'

I looked at her. 'Like what?'

'Like those awful people. Those awful dead people at that hospital.' She paused. 'I knew you'd decide to be all right again.'

This short dialogue offers a lot of information very briefly – in particular about the mother, who has no idea of what Esther has suffered in and out of hospital and why she cannot face more therapy. Esther's mother clearly misunderstands the nature of mental illness and sees it as a stigma – 'those awful dead people'. She obviously thinks that Esther has been play-acting – 'I knew you'd decide to be all right'. In short, she does not know her daughter, her 'baby', at all, and doesn't seem to grasp or to care that Esther has suffered so much.

It also reveals some information about Esther: she tries to communicate with her mother but fails, and realises that there is no real communication between them – 'I looked at her'.

So what does this short extract of dialogue achieve?

- It reminds you of what has happened earlier.

- It summarises, accurately and briefly, the relationship between Esther and her mother.

- It gives a surprisingly clear picture of the poor quality of the mothering offered to Esther.

- The simplicity of the style helps the reader to know the speaker, Esther, and to get a picture of how she responds to people.

ACTIVITY 27

Select a piece of dialogue from the text you are studying, or work with the Jane Gardam extract here. Analyse how the author uses the dialogue to convey important ideas, and discuss the style in which it is written. Use the above models for guidance.

This extract is from a short story called 'The Kiss of Life', from Jane Gardam's collection *The Pangs of Love*. The story is about a trio of relationships between two elderly ladies, Edna and Mew, and a store manager, Mr Paterson. Here Edna and Mew speak to each other for the first time:

> 'You're not meant to touch the peaches,' said large Edna, [. . .]
>
> 'I was just smelling it,' said Mew, rather frightened and not truthful, for she had in fact been touching it, too, and had been about to put it against her face to touch it more.
>
> 'It's not sanitary,' said Edna. 'It's the way colds get passed. By touch. You'll have to buy it now. You can't put it back.'
>
> 'Won't she?' she asked an assistant running by with papers on a clip-board.

What do you learn about Edna here, and what do you learn about Mew? What do you think this exchange indicates about their future relationship?

Narrative viewpoint

Narrative viewpoint is the point of view from which the author allows the reader to perceive the events within the text. There are several ways of varying this, including first-person narration, third-person narration, the use of a child's viewpoint, split narrative and the use of letters.

First-person narration

Here the central or another character tells the story through his or her own eyes. Charlotte Bronte uses first-person narration in her novel *Jane Eyre*, which begins and ends with Jane speaking to the reader directly:

> There was no possibility of taking a walk that day [. . .] My Edward and I, then, are happy: [. . .]

This type of narration achieves several effects. As you read, you feel close to the person telling the story and build up a relationship with this character, in this case Jane; you feel you get to know her from the inside. You also recognise her language, which gives the book unity of tone. But is there too much from one point of view? You will see that in books that use this method of narration, authors incorporate many other devices to offer different viewpoints.

When authors write in the first person they allow you to see into the minds of characters as they are in the process of thinking, which is sometimes called **interior monologue**. You have already looked at an example of this through the thoughts of Charles Arrowby in Iris Murdoch's *The Sea, The Sea* (page 21).

Third-person narrative

This is the standard form of many novels in which the author is recounting the lives of the characters. Take Thomas Hardy's *Tess of the d'Urbervilles*, the story of the sad life of Tess. It begins with descriptions of several characters, focusing in on Tess as she dances on the village green. Even though it uses third-person narrative we still get to know Tess's inner thoughts, because Hardy tells us them:

> Tess stole a glance at her husband. He was pale, even tremulous; but as before, she was appalled by the determination revealed in the depths of this gentle being she had married [. . .]

Hardy lets you know exactly what is going on in Tess's head. In fact, using the third-person narrative technique gives the author great freedom, because he does not have to write in the voice of one character all the time, or use the same register throughout. But don't be fooled into thinking that the author is letting the story tell itself. He can control his characters in a god-like way, and often intervenes to influence our responses to a character or to a situation. Hardy has a massive sympathy for Tess, and interrupts the narration of the tale to address the reader at times, perhaps most famously after Tess has been hanged:

> 'Justice' was done, and the President of the Immortals, in Aeschylean phrase, had ended his sport with Tess.

Hardy influences us as readers in several ways. He firmly places Tess as a victim to make sure that she has our sympathies. The reference to Aeschylus is important: Aeschylus was a great Greek writer of tragedies, in which man has no control over his life but is ruled by cruel gods; again, this helps us to see Tess as a victim who has little chance of controlling her life. Notice that Hardy places the word 'justice' in quotation marks, to let us know that we are to query this word. He intends you to pick up sarcasm or **irony** here, as what happens to Tess is not to be considered just.

ACTIVITY 28

Examine your chosen text, and decide which narrative form the writer has chosen to use. If it is the third-person form, carefully look through the book for any cases where you think that the writer has intervened to break the narrative account and lead the reader into forming an opinion.

Writing from the viewpoint of a child

A child's viewpoint can create interesting effects in prose texts. L. P. Hartley uses this technique in his novel *The Go-Between*. In this extract, young Leo, the central character, is dragged along by the lady of the manor, Mrs Maudsley, until he sees his 'friends' having sex:

Not a sound came from the forlorn row of huts; only the rain pattering on their battered roofs. I could not bear to aid her in her search, and shrank back, crying. 'No, you *shall* come,' she said, and seized my hand, and it was then that we saw them, together on the ground, the Virgin and the Water-Carrier, two bodies moving like one. I think I was more mystified than horrified; it was Mrs. Maudsley's repeated screams that frightened me, and a shadow on the wall that opened and closed like an umbrella.

ACTIVITY 29

Work out the ways in which Hartley achieves effects in this extract. You should think about: the use of adjectives like 'forlorn' and 'battered'; the child's attitude ('crying', 'mystified' and 'frightened') and his innocence (his image of the 'umbrella'); and the awareness of the reader compared to that of the child.

Split narrative account

Some writers may use a split narrative account, where the story is told through the eyes and voice of more than one speaker. An example of this is Graham Greene's novel *The End of the Affair*, in which the author writes about the problems of the Catholic religion. The two central characters, Bendrix and Sarah, are having an affair. They are together when a bomb drops on their building, and it looks as though Bendrix has been killed. Sarah prays and promises God that if her lover survives she will end the affair. The reader sees the first part of the book through the eyes of Bendrix, who is hurt, baffled and bewildered because Sarah has left him. Then in the second part the same events are seen through Sarah's eyes; Greene reveals why she made the pact, and why she cannot continue the affair.

What are the advantages of this technique? The reader always knows more than the characters do about what is going on – a form of **dramatic irony** – so is in a better position than the characters themselves to understand situations. You get to know the minds of the characters very intimately. There is also a great unity of action, characters and events; the novel hangs together tightly, as there is always an overview.

ACTIVITY 30

Rewrite an episode from your text through the eyes of another character.

Remember that character is established and defined by:

- what a character says

- what a character does

- differences between what a character says and does

- how other characters react to this character

- the language used in the account of this character: is it positive or negative?

- analysing the character's interior monologues.

ACTIVITY 31

Using this checklist, compile a character study from your set text, or look again at any character studies that you may have compiled.

Letters

Letters offer another way of varying viewpoints. You have already seen this approach at work in Alice Walker's novel *The Color Purple*, which is written in the form of letters (page 4), and in Ian McEwan's novel *Enduring Love*, which concludes with a letter from one character to another (page 24). Letters allow the reader to see events from different angles.

Setting

Setting is always important in establishing the structure of a novel or short story. You become familiar with settings, especially if they are revisited throughout a book, and gain an understanding of a character's relationships with the setting in which they are placed.

Sometimes an author describes the setting vividly to give a feeling of reality to the book. Here is an example taken from Iris Murdoch's novel *The Bell*. One of the central characters, Dora, goes out into the gardens:

They went on down to the causeway. This crossed the lake in a series of shallow arches built of old brick which had weathered to a rich blackish red. Each arch with its reflection made a dark ellipse. Dora noticed that the centre of the causeway was missing and had been replaced by a wooden section standing on piles.

Here you are offered a clear picture of the lake in the gardens of the community's home. There is a sense of richness in the idea of the brick 'weathering'; it seems solid and secure. There is a vivid reflection in the water, which suggests stillness and tranquillity. You have a sense of deep colours, black and brick red, but the author does more than establish a sense of place here; this setting becomes central to the later dramatic events of the novel. So Murdoch uses setting to foreshadow events, the red and black relating to the murder and passion that will follow.

In other words, when a writer establishes settings, they are usually more than a mere backdrop to events. As you become familiar with the settings, you pick up associations that remind you, in another sort of shorthand, about the themes of the book. Here is an example from Emily Bronte's novel *Wuthering Heights*. There are two opposed families and family homes in this novel. Here is an account of the Earnshaw home:

Wuthering Heights is the name of Mr. Heathcliff's dwelling. 'Wuthering' being a significant provincial adjective, descriptive of the atmospheric tumult to which its station is exposed in stormy weather. Pure, bracing ventilation they must have up there at all times, indeed; one may guess the power of the north wind blowing over the edge, by the excessive slant of a few stunted firs at the end of the house; and by a range of gaunt thorns all stretching their limbs one way, as if craving alms of the sun.

What do you gather from this description of setting? Immediately, the house is linked to the central character, Heathcliff, and its qualities are those that you come to associate with Heathcliff himself. The house is comfortless, cold and exposed to 'tumults' of weather, which will become the merciless passions that Heathcliff imposes on his fellow inmates. The firs are *stunted*, unnatural, as Heathcliff's own feelings are revealed to be, and the thorns seem to be begging from the sun, just as some of the characters will later beg for mercy from Heathcliff. In other words, setting is used as a shorthand to develop your perception of character. When you read of Wuthering Heights, you always think of these cruel qualities of Heathcliff.

Here is an account of Thrushcross Grange, the other home in *Wuthering Heights*. This is where the Lintons live, a family that is in many ways the opposite of the Heathcliff family:

Both of us were able to look in by standing on the basement, and clinging to the ledge, and we saw – ah! it was beautiful – a splendid place carpeted with crimson, and crimson-covered chairs and tables, and a pure white ceiling bordered by gold, a shower of glass-drops hanging in silver chains from the centre, and shimmering with little soft tapers.

ACTIVITY 32

Using the previous analysis of Heathcliff's home as a model, work out what Emily Bronte is suggesting about the family who live at Thrushcross Grange.

Setting is also used to establish a mood. Here is an extract from William Trevor's novel *Death in Summer*, in which Thaddeus Davenant, one of the central characters, is remembering the setting of his wife's funeral:

All that is over now, and yet is coldly there in the first moment of waking every day: the coffin, the flowers laid out, the bright white surplice of the clergyman, dust to dust [. . .] The day the heatwave began it was, that funeral afternoon, the empty blue of the sky touched upon in the clergyman's brief eulogy.

This writing is deceptively clear and artless. There are the key aspects of the funeral scene in a series of brief memory flashes: the sky, an 'empty blue', economically tells us of Thaddeus's feelings after his wife's death, as he is empty also. The weather is linked to the day of her funeral. The word order is natural, 'The day the heatwave began it was', rather jumbled as suits a man whose mind is troubled.

But there is a trick here. William Trevor is deliberately misleading the reader, lulling us to an unthinking acceptance of what the writer shows us. In fact, the mood is to be reversed as murder is uncovered. So here setting is used to mislead and deceive the reader in order to set up a shock effect later in the book.

ACTIVITY 33

Make sure that you have a list of the various settings used in your chosen text. You can now begin to analyse their significance.

Use of repetition

Just as a novel's settings begin to have associations for you as you read, many writers use repetition or repetitive motifs in a similar way, to provide a brief memory flash that illuminates the themes of the novel or short story.

A **motif** is like a refrain in music, a series of images or symbols that recur throughout a text. Here are a few examples.

In his novel *The Scarlet Letter*, Nathaniel Hawthorne uses several repetitive motifs, including the letter 'A' and the colours black and red. The central character, Hester Prynne, has been accused of adultery, and has to wear this letter on her breast. Gradually, as you read through the novel, your associations change. You realise her goodness, and the 'A' with its associations of adultery changes to include the 'A' of angel. The colour red, as in roses, is always linked to Hester, which may remind you every time you read the word of her passionate nature. The colour black is always linked to Arthur Dimmesdale, and as the novel progresses you realise that this colour suits his character; he is hard and cold, a complete contrast to Hester.

In *Tess of the d'Urbervilles*, Thomas Hardy links the colour red to Tess in much the same way. She has a red ribbon in her hair when we first see her; her lips are a luscious red; she is pictured with red strawberries in her mouth and down the bodice of her dress. The effect is similar: we are reminded of Tess's beauty, passion and sexuality whenever we read of this colour.

Here's a final example from Ken Kesey's novel *One Flew Over the Cuckoo's Nest*. Kesey makes the Chief, his narrator, use a series of repetitive motifs. As you encounter these motifs you come to realise their intended associations: the 'fog' means the heavy drug treatments imposed on the inmates; the 'machinery' is the hospital system at work; the 'Combine' is society, working against the interests of the patients. So whenever you read one of these repeated words, the themes of the novel are brought to mind.

A C T I V I T Y 3 4

Carefully check through your selected text to see whether the author uses repetition. If yes, work out the sequence of motifs, and the associations they suggest to you. Here are some examples: the use of music in *A Clockwork Orange*; references to the river in *Huckleberry Finn*; and references to nature and colour in *Wuthering Heights*.

Working with time

Time can be difficult to handle, though it is often straightforward in novels and short stories where the narrative is broadly realistic and follows a natural chronological sequence. But how do writers cope in those types of prose that move backwards and forwards through time? There are two interesting ways of departing from traditional chronological sequencing: flashbacks and time shifts.

Flashback

In the commonest form of flashback, the author makes a character reminisce about events that happened in the past; this takes us backwards in time without disturbing the flow of the narrative. Here is a remarkable example from the novel *The Child in Time* by Ian McEwan. The central character, Stephen, glances through the window of a pub and sees two people inside:

But the young man and woman were engrossed. He gulped his beer, a pint to her half, and talked earnestly, while her drink remained untouched. [. . .] His legs weakened, a chill spread downwards through his stomach. He was looking into the eyes of the woman, and he knew who she was. [. . .] There was no response from the young woman who he knew, beyond question, was his mother. She could not see him. She was listening to his father speak [. . .]

Here there is a flashback, but a flashback presented in dramatic terms as a real experience. Stephen is made to confront his past imaginatively, but also as if it had really happened. The window he looks through is not just the pub window; it is the window of time. He sees his parents when they were young, before he had been conceived. It is as if the author is telling us that the past is always with us.

Joseph Heller in his novel *Catch-22* uses flashback in a complex way. The central character of the novel, Yossarian, appears to be mentally ill when you first encounter him. He does not want to return to war as a bombardier, and he may even be cowardly. Heller introduces a series of flashbacks that Yossarian has, related to the death of his fellow crew member Snowden. As the sequence of the same flashback builds up, you begin to realise that there is something important hidden here. In the final flashback of the sequence, near the end of the book, you discover the grim details of Snowden's death:

Yossarian ripped open the snaps of Snowden's flak suit and heard himself scream wildly as Snowden's insides slithered down to the floor in a soggy pile and just kept dripping out.

ACTIVITY 35

Work out the effects achieved by this flashback. You may want to consider the reason for Yossarian's state of mind, and how this flashback affects your response to him. How does Heller use language to achieve particular effects?

Time shift

Time shift is similar to flashback but works in a slightly different way and for slightly different purposes. Here's an example from Kate Atkinson's novel *Behind the Scenes at the Museum*. At the end of the book, Ruby Lennox revisits the shop in York where she spent so much time in her childhood. She glances out of the window of the shop, which is now a café:

From one of the newly-genteel lace-curtained windows I can see a wild scene in the street below – the stomping, disciplined marching of thousands of feet as a Roman army marches up from the river, through the *porta praetoria* and along the street. The plumes on the centurions' helmets tremble, the standard bearers hold their standards proudly aloft.

Without warning, and still writing in the present tense, Atkinson has pushed back the time by over a thousand years. Her point is that this is life: we all arrive, we live, and then we disappear into the museum of history. The only difficulty with this technique is that on first reading it can be confusing; but it is a vivid and dramatic way of including the past in a novel.

This sort of confusion may be evident when you first read Toni Morrison's novel *Beloved*. Here, time shift is used to move backwards and forwards through time and history as the writer explores the damage caused by slavery to people of a later generation. In one of the central parts of the novel you discover the secret guilt of the central character, Sethe, and how it causes the haunting by the child, Beloved. The piece comes unexpectedly and shockingly, beginning:

> When the four horsemen came – schoolteacher, one nephew, one slave catcher and a sheriff – the house on Bluestone Road was so quiet they thought they were too late. [. . .]
>
> Inside, two boys bled in the sawdust and dirt at the feet of a nigger woman holding a blood-soaked child to her chest with one hand and an infant by the heels in the other. She did not look at them; she simply swung the baby towards the wall planks, missed and tried to connect a second time [. . .]

ACTIVITY 36

Using the extract from *Beloved*, work out the effects of a sudden time shift. You may want to include: the dramatic effects achieved by the author's use of language; the economy of being able to avoid lengthy chronological narrative prose; and the development of the author's ideas. Could there be a suggestion that the past is always with us and is inescapable?

Although the reader may experience initial difficulties in understanding time shifts, they are sorted out on deeper acquaintance with the book. The vividness of the effect makes the effort to understand well worth it.

ACTIVITY 37

Look again at your chosen text and see how the writer treats past events. Perhaps there is a mixture of devices used. If so, what effect does each one have?

This concludes your work on the third Assessment Objective. There is a series of questions that you could ask yourself about the prose style of the set text you are reading:

- Is the style clear or complex?

- Is the writing subjective or objective?

- Is the style traditional, or modern or experimental?

- What about word order and pacing?

- How is dialogue used?

- Is there much use of figurative language? Why?

- Does the work involve impressionistic or psychological analysis?

- How is the past handled?

- What form of narrative account is used?

In the novel, the writer has plenty of time to develop the ideas. The short story is a much more condensed form of prose, which naturally affects the form, so if you are reading a sequence of short stories, you may well include a few other questions:

- Does the author use poetic language to overcome the constraints of length?

- How are the short stories in a selection related to each other?

- Are they linked by theme, place, the author's concerns and style?

- Does the author provide any sort of framing device, as in Jane Gardam's *The Pangs of Love*, in which a frame is provided by 'The First Adam' and 'The Last Adam'?

You are now able to respond fully to the three questions relating to the first three Assessment Objectives. If you remember, these were:

- What ideas is the writer trying to convey to readers?

- What experience or experiences is the writer trying to convey?

- How is the writer trying to convey these ideas?

You can now answer this third question by demonstrating a detailed understanding of the ways in which authors express the ideas they are trying to convey.

Assessment Objectives 4 and 5i

Your in-depth look at the third Assessment Objective explored the ways in which prose texts are written. This also means that you have now covered the first Assessment Objective, through the introduction to various technical devices and the associated terms. These two Assessment Objectives carry the heaviest weighting, being worth 20 out of the 35 marks available in this module, so you are well on the way to achieving decent marks.

You have also spent time on acquiring the 'knowledge and understanding' required by the second Assessment Objective, which is worth another 5 marks;

this module will be completed when you finish your work on the final two Assessment Objectives, AO4 and AO5i.

There is no reason to feel worried or anxious about these last two Objectives. Remember: this module is an introduction to the study of literature, so the last two Objectives are weighted lightly and carry 5 marks each. At this stage in your studies, the text is the thing; you are not expected to spend precious study time reading 'secondary' texts that explore your novel or short story. Nor are you expected to read books of literary critical theory, or books that explore at length different critical readings of your text.

Assessment Objective 4

AO4 requires that you 'articulate independent opinions and judgements, informed by different interpretations of literary texts by other readers'. The Objective breaks naturally into two parts: 'independent opinions and judgements', and 'different interpretations of literary texts by other readers'.

Try to focus your work in this module on these three areas, which you may examine in turn:

- the formulation of your own independent opinion about your text

- the awareness of ambiguity in your text, and

- the awareness of different readings of your texts, in which different interpretations are formulated and established by textual evidence.

The formulation of your own independent opinion

You may well be asked in the examination 'Why do you think . . .?', or 'How far do you agree . . .?', or 'How far do you think . . .?' The important thing to note about these types of question is that the examiner is asking you for an opinion, so you must respond by offering an opinion or judgement.

This is one way in which the fourth Assessment Objective may be tested. If you fail to offer an opinion or try to hedge your bets – for example, by saying 'I'm not sure . . .', or 'It is not clear . . .' – you fail to respond to the set task and risk losing the five marks on offer. When you go into the examination, always be confident that you do have a firm opinion about what the book means to you.

The awareness of ambiguity in your text

Remember that texts don't have a single meaning. The author may have created deliberate ambiguity, or may have intended the reader to form a certain opinion, but when you, the reader, come to the text you bring a different set of experiences and associations to the interpretation. Often, you may derive a different message from the text, and not the one that the author intended – but your interpretation is always acceptable as long as you can back up your reading by textual evidence.

Here is an example of ambiguity for you to consider. The extract is from E. M. Forster's novel *A Passage to India*. In this passage, an English woman, Miss Quested, has made a trip led by Aziz to the Marabar caves. This is a new departure from the comfortable colonial club life of the English in India. She is horrified at her experience there:

Bending their heads, they disappeared one by one into the interior of the hills. The small black hole gaped where their varied forms and colours had momentarily functioned [. . .] Bland and bald rose the precipices [. . .] she had always suffered from faintness, and the cave had become too full [. . .] She lost Aziz in the dark, didn't know who touched her, couldn't breathe, and some vile naked thing struck her face and settled on her mouth like a pad.

ACTIVITY 38

a) Working in groups, analyse the ways in which Forster conveys the experience of being in the caves. You may include:

- the choice of verbs and the effects of these verbs

- the choice of adjectives and the effectiveness of these

- the punctuation.

b) Then discuss any ambiguities which you may find. You may consider:

- whether Miss Quested feels claustrophobic or faint

- whether she has difficulties in coping with new or strange experiences

- whether there are any sexual implications. Could there be any Freudian significance in the choice of language such as 'Bland and bald rose the precipices', 'the small black hole', or 'some vile naked thing struck her face and settled on her mouth'?

- any other interpretations you may find.

ACTIVITY 39

Select an episode from your set text and work in groups to discuss any ambiguities that you may find.

The awareness of different readings of your text . . .

This third area raises further issues. One is that different readers or groups of readers will respond to texts differently. For example, Salman Rushdie's book *The Satanic Verses* caused no problem to non-Islamic readers, who saw it as a witty, satirical book; but it caused great offence to Islamic readers, who saw the book as a sacrilegious attack on the Koran. The reaction was so strong that Rushdie was seen as a heretic, and was condemned to be killed by a member of the Islamic faith.

Interpretations of a book can also change over time. A fairly recent example is *The Child in Time* by Ian McEwan. This was published more than a decade ago, at a time when its most likely interpretation was as an exploration of childhood, of relationships with parents and friends, and of how the passing of time affects our perceptions of life. Initially, the concern with time and the treatment of time were of great interest to readers. But in the years since its publication there have been many problems with 'sleaze' in politics. For this reason, it may be that readers now see its satire on political life as the most important aspect of the book. McEwan mocks the childlike or self-serving behaviour of politicians; he also satirises the peculiar and irrational actions of the obsessive members of a secret service called the Movement.

You may also become aware of changes that have occurred through time in a reading of *Jane Eyre*. Do you see Jane as a heroine of splendid moral virtues who gets her reward, whereas others get their comeuppance? She marries the lord of the manor; he is afflicted with blindness almost as a punishment. Or do you read the book as an attack on the wealthy who are indifferent to the poor? Aunt Reed has no charity, and the owner of the school, Mr Brocklehurst, starves his pupils whilst feasting with his family. Then again you could read *Jane Eyre* in a modern sense, as an early feminist book supporting and applauding the actions of a brave, independent woman who stubbornly makes her own life as teacher, governess and finally wife.

You may find it helpful at this point to look at some of the more important schools of critical interpretative thought. Here, there is a brief examination of the feminist, socialist or Marxist, and Freudian ways of reading texts.

Feminist readings

Feminist interpreters look at the main arguments of a text in terms of claims about the rights of women and their roles in society.

You have looked already at several examples of work that could be regarded as feminist, such as the novels of Alice Walker, Toni Morrison, and the example of *Jane Eyre* above. Other female feminist writers include Angela Carter and Margaret Atwood.

Angela Carter's novel *The Magic Toyshop* may be seen to offer a feminist exploration of a young girl's rite of passage from adolescence to womanhood and her developing awareness of her own sexuality as a source of power and life-enriching experience. In her short story sequence *Bloody Chamber*, Carter rewrites traditional fairy tales, giving them a feminist reading by criticising the stereotypical male attitudes that she believes lie behind these stories.

Margaret Atwood likewise writes books that we could perceive as being feminist. In *The Handmaid's Tale*, she explores the lives of women who are deprived of their rights and roles in life. More recently she wrote *Cat's Eye*; on the surface this appears to be about a victim called Elaine Risley, who is bullied at school by a group of pupils led by Cordelia. However, this book may also be read in feminist terms as a general exploration of how women become victims in society. The image of the cat's eye, first of all a marble, is repeated throughout the novel, gathering associations as it reappears. Finally, you realise that Elaine herself has taken on these cat-like qualities. She learns the cat's instinct for survival as she gets through nasty situations, using up her nine lives, and she also develops the cat's eye ability to see in the dark – she peers back through the darkness and confusion of the past to make sense of her life, and understands herself as she is at the beginning and the end of the book, a successful painter. To achieve this, Elaine had to come to terms with, and overcome, the traditional expectations of female roles in society.

Along the way there are some clear attacks on male chauvinism and macho attitudes:

> When they've had several beers they might talk about women. They refer to their girlfriends, some of whom live with them; these are called 'my old lady'. Or they make jokes about the models in Life Drawing, who change from night to night. They speak of going to bed with them, as if this depends only on their inclination or lack of it. There are two possible attitudes to this: lip-smacking or nauseating revulsion. 'A cow,' they say. 'A bag.' 'What a discard.' Sometimes they do this with an eye towards me, looking to see how I will take it.

ACTIVITY 40

Analyse the ways in which Atwood presents the men's attitudes here, and how you may be led to think that she is critical of their attitudes. You might consider: the ways in which the men amuse themselves; their attitudes towards women; and the ways in which their language and preoccupations reveal their attitudes.

It is not just female writers who defend the roles and value of women in society. Shakespeare, in his portrayal of women such as Portia in *The Merchant of Venice*, could be seen as the equivalent of a modern feminist. In his novel *Catch-22*, Joseph Heller attributes a positive value to women such as Nately's whore and the nurse.

Socialist and Marxist interpretations

Socialist and similar interpretations rest on attitudes to class structure and behaviour. You have already seen comments on *Jane Eyre* in socialist terms, in which a sympathy could be felt for the poor orphan. Marxist interpretations rest more specifically on the idea that wealth should be redistributed to help the poor; again, you have already seen George Orwell's novel *Down and Out in Paris and London* interpreted in this way, and the same approach could be applied to Charles Dickens's novel *Hard Times*. Dickens is critical of the wealth amassed by factory owners such as Mr Bounderby, wealth that is not shared with the poor. (As his name suggests, Bounderby goes beyond the bounds of decent behaviour.) Gradgrind's bad educational system, which is indeed grindingly dull and limited in its insistence upon facts only, and Harthouse's politics also conspire to keep the poor in the wretched conditions they endure in Coketown:

It was a town of red brick, or of brick that would have been red if the smoke and ashes had allowed it; but as matters stood it was a town of unnatural red and black like the painted face of a savage. It was a town of machinery and tall chimneys, out of which interminable serpents of smoke trailed themselves for ever and ever, and never got uncoiled. It had a black canal in it, and a river that ran purple with ill-smelling dye, and vast piles of building full of windows where there was a rattling and a trembling all day long, and where the piston of the steam-engine worked monotonously up and down like the head of an elephant in a state of melancholy madness.

ACTIVITY 41

Analyse the ways in which Dickens presents this picture of Coketown. Using the skills you have now acquired, you should include: the ways in which he uses figurative language; his use of colour and of the senses; and the possibility that Coketown could be compared to hell. What do these factors reveal about Dickens's attitudes towards society?

Freudian or psychological readings

Freudian interpretations rest on the idea of psychoanalysis of the subconscious mind. You have already seen an example of this in the sexual interpretation of Miss Quested's visit to the Marabar caves. There may be a Freudian reading of an episode in *Jane Eyre*. As an adolescent, in the second chapter of the novel, Jane is locked in the red room as a punishment. She herself comments 'my blood was still warm'. Overstressed, she faints. According to Freudian commentators this indicates the onset of her periods and menstrual cycle.

ACTIVITY 42

This is the most important aspect of this section. Working in groups, try to draw out as many interpretations or readings from your text as possible. In pairs, look for different meanings to find evidence for the points you make from your text.

Presenting your opinions and judgements

In the examination, you may be asked whether you agree with a given reading, interpretation or comment about the text; or you may be offered two opinions or interpretations and asked which you prefer. You may be asked to consider why a text could appeal to a certain group of readers or, quite simply, to express an opinion or judgement of your own.

Remember: there are three aspects to consider when addressing the fourth Assessment Objective:

- be confident in holding and expressing an opinion or judgement

- be aware of ambiguities of meaning, character or situation in your text, and

- be aware of different interpretations or readings of your text.

It is now time to turn to the fifth and final Assessment Objective. But first, review these three further questions that you can now ask about a text:

- How do I respond to the author's ideas?

- Do I agree with what the author is saying?

- Can I find more, perhaps several other, readings of the text?

Assessment Objective 5i

AO5i requires that you 'show understanding of the contexts in which literary texts are written and understood'. As with AO4, there is no need to feel concerned or worried about this Objective. You are not expected at this early stage in your studies to read books around your central text. In our introduction to this book we looked at the various types of context that you will eventually consider. In this module, you need only concern yourself with three of these contexts:

- the period or era, including significant social, historical, political and cultural processes

- the work in terms of the writer's milieu or environment

- a specific passage set against the work from which it is taken – a part-to-whole context.

What are contexts?

The simplest answer is that literary **contexts** are two sets of frames, the outer and the inner. The contexts you need to consider for AS level are generally the inner contexts, concerns developed within the text itself.

A writer may develop a social frame within the text to explore aspects of society such as love or marriage, faith, or social behaviour and morality. Or the inner context could be political, with enquiries into political behaviour, or legal, with exploration of matters such as justice. You can see that within the frame of reference that the author constructs through the narrative, you are back with familiar ideas of exploring themes or concerns.

You will not be asked to explore a text's outer frames or contexts in any great detail. Outer contexts include the ways in which the text relates externally to matters of genre, biography, other works by the same author, or the development of language use over time.

If you do need to make a reference to an external context, it would be brief and accessible. An example here is the need to understand the American Dream when reading *The Great Gatsby*, or the sort of knowledge you may well have had at GCSE in order to understand Lennie's and George's behaviour in Steinbeck's novel *Of Mice and Men*. Another example is the understanding about history needed to explore Orwell's *Animal Farm* or Watson's *Talking in Whispers*. You don't have to go outside your text for an in-depth study of any external context until you get to A2 level.

When you are asked in the examination to discuss context, the examiner always has to make it clear precisely what sort of context you are expected to write about. For example, if you were to study *A Clockwork Orange* you may be asked to write about brutality in society. This targets the first sort of context, that of a period or era including significant social, historical, political and cultural processes.

The period or era

This is the context that most often occurs in the exam, as it concerns society and the events that the author is concerned about. It covers a very long list that includes all the social aspects of poverty, education, women's role in society, violence, war, sexuality, injustice, marriage, and love. This context involves all of the texts offered for study.

An example of a social and moral context is found in Mark Twain's *Huckleberry Finn*, where the writer is concerned with the immorality of society. In *Beloved*, Toni Morrison is concerned with slavery, a historical context that is also political and cultural. An example of a political context is Ian McEwan's interest in the actions of politicians and the Movement in *The Child in Time*.

Here is an extract from Chapter 21 of Chinua Achebe's novel *Things Fall Apart*. The missionaries have settled in this particular part of Africa and their presence has brought about many changes. This has upset the old Chief, Okonkwo:

The new religion and government and the trading stores were very much in the people's eyes and minds. There were still many who saw these new institutions as evil, but even they talked and thought about little else [. . .]

Okonkwo was deeply grieved. And it was not just a personal grief. He mourned for the clan, which he saw breaking up and falling apart, [. . .]

ACTIVITY 43

Try to work out the possible contexts in this extract. These are the points of interest: (1) there has obviously been great change in the area; (2) people are reacting differently, and their attitudes and values are changing; and (3) Okonkwo represents the old order, which is being overthrown. What contexts do these represent?

Here are some of the contexts: (1) suggests a social and historical context; (2) also indicates social contexts, with the concern for attitudes and values; and (3) clearly expresses the historical and cultural context, as things are falling apart for the old tribes in a period of historical change.

ACTIVITY 44

Explore your set text, and list examples of the contexts you find there.

The work in terms of the writer's biography or milieu

It is unlikely that matters of biography will be relevant to your work in this module for two reasons. First, the study of a writer's biography or life would take you well outside the study of your text. Second, experienced examiners know that questions relating to biography take candidates away from giving answers about the text into vaguer areas involving guesswork at links between biography and the text.

However, you may be asked to consider the writer's milieu. This is taken to mean the people with whom the writer had a personal acquaintance, or ideas of the period that affected the writer. Examples include Ian McEwan's interest in the theory of predestination and the influence of this on *Enduring Love*, and Mary Shelley's interest in the science of her day and its appearance in *Frankenstein*.

You may have spotted overlaps in the internal or social contexts. You may also have noticed that at times Assessment Objectives 4 and 5i overlap: for example, women's issues and feminism, Marxism and class, and Freudian analysis, which we discussed under the heading of Assessment Objective 4, are in themselves contexts and areas of concern for some writers. How do you distinguish between the two objectives? Quite simply:

- AO4 always relates to interpretation, and therefore to the reader

- AO5i relates to the ideas in the text, and therefore to the writer and the writer's use of inner and outer contexts to transmit ideas.

Part-to-whole relationships

This is another context that you may well encounter in your examination. You must remember that this is an open-book examination, so you are allowed to take your texts into the examination. For this reason, the setting of an extract is a good way to trigger you into writing a response.

Sometimes you are given the beginning of a novel or short story, and asked how it is used to introduce ideas; or you are given the ending, and asked whether it forms a satisfactory conclusion to the piece; or you are given a passage that is significant in some way. The point to remember here is that if you are asked to use an extract as a 'starting point' or to 'begin with considerations of', you must always consider both the extract and the whole text, or you are not responding properly to the aspect of context and may lose your marks.

ACTIVITY 45

Pick out a key passage from your text, and work out the ways in which it relates to the ideas of the whole novel.

You have now discovered four points about contexts:

- There is series of outer contexts or frames surrounding every piece of literature.

- There are inner frames or contexts within each work.

- There will probably be several contexts within each work.

- These contexts may well overlap.

As a closing activity for this section, look at a couple of extracts from Joseph Heller's novel *Catch-22*. In the first of these the central character Yossarian has taken unofficial leave and is in Rome just after the city has been bombed. The chapter is called 'The Eternal City':

Rome was in ruins, he saw, when the plane was down. The airdrome had been bombed eight months before, and knobby slabs of white stone had been bulldozed into flat-topped heaps on both sides of the entrance through the wire fence surrounding the field. The Colosseum was a dilapidated shell, and the Arch of Constantine had fallen. Nately's whore's apartment was a shambles. The girls were gone, and the only one there was the old woman. [. . .] She was talking aloud to herself when Yossarian entered and began moaning as soon as she saw him.

'Gone.'

'Who?'

'All. All the poor young girls.'

What sort of, and how many, contexts can we deduce from this extract?

1   There is the context of war, Rome has been bombed.

2   There is a historical context with the reference to the Colosseum and the Arch, which both relate to ancient Rome and remind us that war is always evident in human history. Is this why the chapter is called 'The Eternal City'?

3   There is the context of morality in the reference to Nately's whore. How have the soldiers been behaving?

4   There is the context of madness and irrationality in the old woman's behaviour. Could this be an image of social madness?

5   There is the social context of society. The young girls have gone as war has diminished and reduced the nature of society. Healthy and vital elements seem to have disappeared.

6   There would be a part-to-whole context if you were able to relate this extract to the rest of the novel.

7   Like Yossarian, Heller was himself involved in the war. This is an example of a context related to the writer's biography or milieu.

ACTIVITY 46

Using the model above, see how many contexts you are able to draw out from the next extract, which is from the same chapter. You may include some of those in the previous list. Yossarian has just seen a young boy being beaten by a man:

One drab woman was weeping silently into a dirty dish towel. The boy was emaciated and needed a haircut. Bright-red blood was streaming from both ears. Yossarian crossed quickly to the other side of the immense avenue to escape the nauseating sight and found himself walking on human teeth lying on the drenched, glistening pavement near splotches of blood kept sticky by the pelting raindrops poking each one like sharp fingernails. [. . .] He circled on tiptoe the grotesque debris and came near a doorway containing a crying soldier holding a saturated handkerchief to his mouth.

Maximising your marks

You should now feel quite confident in handling the last of the Assessment Objectives, which adds two new questions to your list:

- In what ways are the ideas original or valuable or interesting?

- What are the influences behind the author's ideas?

To recap, here is the complete list of questions that you are now in a position to ask yourself when exploring your prose text:

- What ideas is the author trying to convey to the reader?

- What experience or experiences is the author trying to convey?

- How, with a detailed understanding of the ways, has the author tried to convey these ideas?

- How do I respond to the author's ideas?

- Do I agree with what the author is saying?

- Can I find more, perhaps several other, readings of the text?

- In what ways are the ideas original or valuable or interesting?

- What are the influences behind the author's ideas?

Before closing, it might be useful to demonstrate how you can move up the ladder of the marking scheme and achieve as many marks as possible in your examination. Each rung of the ladder represents a mark band or grade, with band 6, the lowest, equivalent to about grade U and band 1 equivalent to an A grade.

Here is an extract from Emily Bronte's *Wuthering Heights*, in which the narrator describes the dead Heathcliff. Imagine that an examination question asks you to compare the presentation of the character Heathcliff in the extract to his presentation in the novel as a whole:

I could not think him dead: but his face and throat were washed with rain; the bedclothes dripped, and he was perfectly still. The lattice, flapping to and fro, had grazed one hand that rested on the sill; no blood trickled from the broken skin, and when I put fingers to it, I could doubt no more: he was dead and stark!

I hasped the window; I combed his long black hair from his forehead; I tried to close his eyes: to extinguish, if possible, that frightful, life-like gaze of exultation before any one else beheld it. They would not shut: they seemed to sneer at my attempts: and his parted lips and sharp white teeth sneered too!

At band 5, a candidate might typically work by using quotation – for example, Heathcliff is 'black' and is related to Hell or to the 'divil'. Candidates in this band would tend to refer to Heathcliff through the use of quotations, without further discussion.

At band 4, the candidate may identify figurative language, such as why and how Heathcliff's eyes and lips were seen to 'sneer'. Candidates here would tend to be accurate in pointing out and naming figurative language, but probably stop short of discussing how these images work and how they are effective.

A candidate at band 3 will probably develop the description by exemplification, and consider other examples in the novel where Heathcliff is 'exultant' or 'sneers', or is like a ghoul, vampire or fiend, adding some discussion of how the images work.

At band 2 there would be some exploration of the presentational ideas and methods. The candidate may discuss how the images of devilry, of exultation and triumph, of the colours black and white work throughout the novel in the presentation of Heathcliff, and how these images are effective in promoting the concerns of the novel.

At band 1, the top band, the presentation of Heathcliff would be analysed conceptually. His 'supernatural' presentation as a devil, for example, may be related to the Heaven/Hell structure of the novel. Elements of his presentation, such as the vampire, may be related to the Gothic form. He would probably be placed in his relation to Nature/strength/depth of love versus society/feebleness/weaker sort of love.

ACTIVITY 47

Select a paragraph of the description of a character or place from your own text. Relate the paragraph to the whole text, working through it at each mark band level using the model above, to see how far up the marking ladder you can move at this stage of your studies.

The examination

You are allowed to take your books into the examination, with highlighting or brief annotation, so don't worry about remembering points of detail or relating extracts to the whole work. You are also given plenty of time for your first examination – one and a half hours to answer one question. This means that you can spend time reading the questions, deciding where the objectives lie behind the questions, and identifying the contexts you have been asked to discuss. You have enough time to choose your question carefully, and there is also time to make a plan.

You now have all the skills necessary for this module, so be confident and do as well as you can.

The Assessment Objectives for this module require that you:

ASSESSMENT OBJECTIVES

The Assessment Objectives for this module require that you:

AO1 communicate clearly the knowledge, understanding and insight appropriate to literary study, using appropriate terminology and accurate and coherent written expression
(5% of the final AS mark; $2^1/_2$% of the final A Level mark)

AO2i respond with knowledge and understanding to literary texts of different types and periods
(10% of the final AS mark; 5% of the final A Level mark)

AO3 show detailed understanding of the ways in which writers' choices of form, structure and language shape meanings
(10% of the final AS mark; 5% of the final A Level mark)

AO5i show understanding of the contexts in which literary texts are written and understood
(10% of the final AS mark; 5% of the final A Level mark)

The structure of the module

The fourth Assessment Objective does not figure here. The module is split into two sections: A (Poetry) and B (Drama). The modern drama element attracts more marks than the poetry component, in line with the scheme shown in the table.

Section	Assessment Objective	Marks
A (poetry)	AO2i	5
	AO3	10
	Total marks for poetry	**15**
B (drama)	AO1	5
	AO2i	5
	AO5i	10
	Total marks for drama	**20**

The examination paper for this module is scaled. The examiners feel that it is not possible to assess candidates and grade their work using only 15 marks for the poetry question and 20 marks for the drama question, so the marks for the paper are doubled. This allows examiners to be more accurate and just in rewarding candidates. The total marks for the paper are then divided back to the original 35 marks to grade the result. You will see these higher mark allocations on your question paper.

Content

This module meets the syllabus's genre requirements for poetry and drama, and also meets the pre-1900 text requirement because all the prescribed poetry is pre-1900.

Section A: Poetry

The Assessment Objectives targeted in this section are AO2i and AO3. You'll automatically acquire 'knowledge and understanding' as you work through this first section of the module, so your focus will be largely on AO3: 'show detailed understanding of the ways in which writers' choices of form, structure and language shape meanings'.

This module approaches the study of poetry using the following sequence:

- the lyric, including the song and the elegy

- metaphysical poetry

- the sonnet

- narrative verse, including Milton's *Paradise Lost*

- aspects of Chaucer's poetry.

Exploring poetry

In many ways, this module begins by building on the skills you acquired during your work on the first module. You should ask yourself some of the same questions that you asked about prose:

- What ideas is the writer trying to convey to the reader?

- What experience or experiences is the writer trying to convey?

- How has the writer used form, structure and language to convey these ideas and experiences?

- In what ways is the poetry original, unusual, valuable or interesting?

The skills you acquired in your preparatory work for the first module provide a useful basis for your study of poetry. You have already begun to consider connotation, association, metaphor, simile, word-order, pacing and ambiguity.

Lyrical poetry

Lyrical poetry is so called because of the musical qualities of the verse, created by the ways in which language, rhyme and rhythm work together. In lyrical poetry, the author expresses his or her own thoughts and feelings, so many forms of poetry come under this broad heading, including the song, the elegy and the sonnet.

The song

The song is traditionally seen as a straightforward form of poetry, with fairly simple language and rhythm. However, this is not always the case.

One of the most famous writers of songs was William Blake, whose *Songs of Innocence and of Experience* were written at the end of the eighteenth century. Blake was very much concerned with religious themes, and in his book he looks at mankind in a state of innocence and then in a state of sin or experience. The poems often fall into pairs; here is an extract from the first poem of one of these pairs, 'The Lamb' and 'The Tyger'.

Little Lamb who made thee
Dost thou know who made thee
Gave thee life & bid thee feed,
By the stream & o'er the mead;
Gave thee clothing of delight,
Softest clothing wooly bright;
Gave thee such a tender voice,
Making all the vales rejoice:
Little Lamb who made thee
Dost thou know who made thee

Knowledge and understanding of the poem (AO2i). The poem is written in a way that suggests a little child is asking a lamb about his creator. The tone is warm and secure; the child describes the lamb with his soft fleecy coat, in the meadows and beside the streams. All is harmonious and gentle.

How the writer expresses these ideas (AO3). Consider the language. All the words are positive: 'life', delight', 'softest', 'bright', 'tender'. No wonder there is rejoicing at this happiness. The use of the soft letters 'l' and 's' creates a quiet tone. But the lamb is also an important image: it represents innocence, and also reminds us that Christ, the son of God, was called a Lamb. God created this son, and he created this kindly universe in which all is well.

The rhythm keeps up the idea of innocence with its simplicity; it is the regular four-stressed line of a children's nursery rhyme or lullaby. And the rhymes are simple, 'thee' occurs twice at the beginning and twice at the end. Why? Could it be to stress simplicity and innocence again? The repetition of the words 'little lamb' works in this way as well. Elsewhere, the rhyme brings together key words that enforce the idea of happiness, such as 'delight' and 'bright'.

Have you noticed the punctuation? It is really rather odd, because there are no question marks after the questions. Why do you think this is? Could this suggest that in this innocent and happy world there is no need to ask questions, because the answer is known: that a kindly God made this perfect world?

The paired poem, 'The Tyger', works as a complete contrast; this poem asks who made the tiger. Here are three of the middle stanzas:

And what shoulder, & what art,
Could twist the sinews of thy heart?
And when thy heart began to beat,
What dread hand? & what dread feet?

What the hammer? what the chain,
In what furnace was thy brain?
What the anvil? what dread grasp,
Dare its deadly terrors clasp?

When the stars threw down their spears
And water'd heaven with their tears:
Did he smile his work to see?
Did he who made the Lamb make thee?

Knowledge and understanding of the poem (AO2i). This is a complete contrast to the first poem. As the lamb represented innocence, the tiger represents a sense of fear and terror. Man has lost his innocence and the perfect world of the first poem has disappeared.

How the poet expresses meaning (AO3). What do you notice about these stanzas? Look at the language. The register is one of violent creation with mechanical tools: 'hammer', 'furnace', 'anvil' all suggest blows, heat and violence in the image of a blacksmith making something mechanical, not alive and loving like the lamb. It is a sort of Frankenstein image. The words are of complete fear: 'dread' is repeated twice in the first stanza of the extract to suggest terror, as though it is too awful to contemplate, too awful to describe, the finished creature. The hard 'd' sound enforces the distressed tone. The creation is not natural, the sinews are twisted. It is an exact reverse of the kindly creation that you saw in the previous poem. The rhymes enforce this: 'beat'/'feet'.

The punctuation of the first stanza sets the tone, with a series of urgent questions that are never answered. Man has lost contact with God, so won't get an answer. The rhythm is the same as in the first poem, but takes on the sound of hammer blows. The punctuation makes the flow of the poem jerky and troubled.

ACTIVITY 1

Beginning where this analysis has left off, finish analysing the other two stanzas in the extract from 'The Tyger'.

You have seen a song of joy and a song of terror. It is time to turn to another type of lyrical poetry, the elegy.

The elegy

Originally, an elegy was a poem written for someone who had died. But this idea has widened to include anyone or anything from the past that has disappeared and is missed.

Here is an extract from an eighteenth-century example of this form, Thomas Gray's poem 'Elegy written in a Country Churchyard':

The curfew tolls the knell of parting day,
    The lowing herd wind slowly o'er the lea,
The ploughman homewards plods his weary way,
    And leaves the world to darkness and to me.

Now fades the glimmering landscape on the sight,
    And all the air a solemn stillness holds,
Save where the beetle wheels his droning flight,
    And drowsy tinklings lull the distant folds;

Knowledge and understanding of the poem (AO2i). What is going on here? Gray presents a vivid picture in words. You see the end of a day in the country. The cattle are quietly mooing as they make their way home; the ploughman is tired after a day's work and is also making his way home. The daylight is fading, all is still. But the poet can see a solitary beetle, and hear the sheep in their folds. The lines, **end-stopped** with commas, make you pause and look at each individual picture.

How the poet expresses meaning (AO3): The language takes the reader further than this picture. The senses of sight and sound are used to make this scene vivid. There is both lightness and darkness, and a metaphorical use of the ploughman leaving the world to darkness as he disappears. The sound of the sheep's bells are making the poet drowsy. The language is mostly plain, and words speak for themselves. Even for the time when this poem was written, the language is old-fashioned, **archaic,** perhaps to call to mind an old landscape painting.

But what about the register? Look at the words 'tolls the knell', 'darkness', 'fades', 'stillness', 'drowsy', 'lull'. These are words that could be the register of approaching death. Perhaps it is not just the death of the day; is it a study of death itself drawing near? The solemn, slow rhythm of the first line, five strong beats, echoes the sound of the funeral bell as a coffin approaches.

Then the poet moves into a section that describes:

> For them no more the blazing hearth shall burn,
> Or busy housewife ply her evening care:
> No children run to lisp their sire's return,
> Or climb his knees the envied kiss to share.
>
> Oft did the harvest to their sickle yield,
> Their furrow oft the stubborn glebe has broke;
> How jocund did they drive their team afield!
> How bow'd the woods beneath their sturdy stroke!

(A sickle is a long scythe-shaped knife used for cutting sheaves of corn; 'glebe' is an old word for a field; and 'jocund' means cheerful.)

ACTIVITY 2

Adopting the model used for the first extract from this poem, analyse the second pair of stanzas to explore how Gray has presented these ideas.

There are other types of elegies that you may encounter. Emily Bronte frequently speaks of past friends and incidents in an elegiac mood. Here are the first and last stanzas from her poem 'Remembrance':

> Cold in the earth – and the deep snow piled above thee,
> Far, far, removed, cold in the dreary grave!
> Have I forgot, my only Love, to love thee,
> Severed at last by Time's all-severing wave?
> . . .
> And, even yet, I dare not let it languish,
> Dare not indulge in memory's rapturous pain;
> Once drinking deep of that divinest anguish,
> How could I seek the empty world again?

In the central stanzas, Emily Bronte repeatedly considers the sense of loss that she has.

Knowledge and understanding of the poem (AO2i). In the first stanza Emily Bronte offers a picture of a cold, lonely and isolated grave. She wonders if she has lost her love for this person.

How the poet expresses meaning (AO3). Emily Bronte's language is deceptively simple, so you need to study it very carefully. Word-order is important. Look at the three key words that begin lines, 'cold', 'far' and 'severed'; immediately Bronte thrusts the main idea at the reader. She uses repetition – 'far' and 'cold' – to enforce the point. The depth of the snow is an image of the intensity of her own feelings and the separation between the two former lovers. The word 'dreary' refers both to the isolated grave and to her own feelings.

The sole image of time as a severed wave is effective. The word 'severed' suggests the suddenness and completeness of death; 'wave' is drawn from natural imagery of the sea. The image calls to mind the irresistible force of death over life, just as sea waves are irresistible and destroy all in their path. This natural imagery is probably the most common type of imagery in Bronte's poems.

The punctuation is also characteristic of Bronte's use of language: the exclamation mark indicates the intensity of her feelings; the question mark, although marking a question to the dead lover, is also aimed at the reader, who is in this way drawn into the poem. At other times she divides the verses with colons or apostrophes, allowing the reader a pause to reflect upon what is being said. The device also mirrors the hesitant pauses of the writer herself as she relives past memories and ponders her thoughts.

ACTIVITY 3

Analyse the final stanza of the poem. Look at the ideas and the use of language, including punctuation.

It is worth remembering that Bronte's tone and mood sometimes change during the course of a poem, so be alert. An example of this is 'How Clear She Shines', which begins as a lyrical song but ends as an elegy.

Metaphysical poetry

The **metaphysical** poets wrote in the seventeenth century, and many readers consider Donne to be the greatest poet of this group. The poems are lyrics in that they are intensely personal; they are also passionate, whether the poet is concerned with the love of a woman or the love of God.

Here is the whole of one of John Donne's love poems, 'The Good-Morrow':

I wonder by my troth, what thou, and I
Did, till we lov'd? were we not wean'd till then?
But suck'd on countrey pleasures, childishly?
Or snorted we i'the seaven sleepers den?
'Twas so; But this, all pleasures fancies bee.
If ever any beauty I did see,
Which I desir'd, and got, 'twas but a dreame of thee.

And now good morrow to our waking soules,
Which watch not one another out of feare;
For love, all love of other sights controules,
And makes one little roome, an every where.
Let sea-discoverers to new worlds have gone,
Let Maps to others, worlds on worlds have showne,
Let us possesse our world, each hath one, and is one.

> My face in thine eye, thine in mine appeares,
> And true plaine hearts doe in the faces rest,
> Where we can finde two better hemispheares
> Without sharpe North, without declining West?
> What ever dyes, was not mixt equally;
> If our two loves be one, or thou and I
> Love so alike, that one doe slacken, none can die.

This poem demonstrates all the central characteristics of metaphysical poetry, as you will see.

Knowledge and understanding of the poem (AO2i). There are three major characteristics of metaphysical poetry evident here.

(1) Evidence of unusual thoughts in ordinary situations: Donne turns an everyday greeting, 'Good morning', into an extraordinary statement and account of his love.

(2) The argument is highly concentrated and sustains a very clear line: in the first stanza Donne asks what either of the lovers knew about pleasure before; in the second stanza he emphasises that the new world the lovers have discovered, their 'little roome', is greater than new worlds found by the discoverers; in the third stanza he proves how solid their love is, but also issues a warning.

(3) Donne explores here the situation of being in love, determined to make the abstract experience as firm and as concrete as possible. He cleverly develops this so that the two lovers who in the first line were 'thou' and 'I' become the 'we' of the last stanza, identical and one.

How the writer expresses meaning (AO3). Again, there are three central characteristics of metaphysical poetry evident in this poem.

(1) Donne uses a startling and striking opening, as he does in much of his poetry. He begins with a direct address to his lover, throwing a challenging sequence of four questions at her.

(2) He uses **conceits**, the startling, typically metaphysical, imagery that works by forcing the reader to see a likeness in things essentially not alike.

Here are some examples of conceits from the poem. In the first stanza Donne thinks of pleasures he has experienced in the past. (There is a crude but playful pun on the words 'suck'd' and 'countrey pleasures' in the sense of sexual activity.) He thinks that all he has experienced in the past were not real pleasures, so he compares them to a 'dreame'. In the second stanza Donne uses two key images: the room, and discoverers. He makes the experience of love so universal, so overwhelming, that it gives the lovers a sense of physical completeness as real as a room; they truly have their own space. This love is more real, more empowering than the discovery of any new physical world. (The word 'let' here is shorthand for 'let us allow that'.)

(3) Donne cleverly uses the conceit to clinch his argument. So in the last stanza he uses an image from physics:

What ever dyes, was not mixt equally;

This conceit means that any compound that is not created from balanced constituents will fail; their love, however, is perfectly balanced and will not fail. Donne then enforces this point in the last line with another clever pun. If, he adds, one or other should 'slacken' in their love, then 'none can die'. The word 'die' also meant to achieve a sexual climax. So in addition to praising their love through the use of the conceit, Donne adds a warning. If love falters, then sexual satisfaction will also fail. It is a double-pronged conclusion, of praise but also of threat.

The imagery, the use of conceits, is not there for simple adornment. In Donne's poetry, as in the other metaphysical poets, the conceit is essential to the argument.

You have explored three aspects of the content of this poem, and three aspects of style. These are the central characteristics of metaphysical verse, and you can apply them to the analysis of most metaphysical poetry.

Here is the first stanza of another of Donne's love poems, 'The Flea':

Marke but this flea, and marke in this,
How little that which thou deny'st me is;
Mee it sucked first, and now sucks thee,
And in this flea, our two bloods mingled bee;
Confesse it, this cannot be said
A sinne, or shame, or losse of maidenhead,
        Yet this enjoyes before it wooe,
        And pamper'd swells with one blood made of two,
        And this, alas, is more than wee would doe.

ACTIVITY 4

The first stanza of 'The Flea' is in a way self-contained, as it presents the argument of the whole poem in brief. Carefully applying the model used for 'The Good-Morrow', analyse this poem. This time you should also look at how the rhyming scheme works to pull together key words.

Later, Donne became Dean of St Paul's. He turned away from writing secular poetry about the love of women, and wrote divine poetry that explored his relationship with God. However, his poetic technique did not change. You'll be able to apply the same method of analysis to both his 'divine' poetry and his love poetry.

The metaphysical poets were always aware of the passing of time, of how human beings have to do all they can in the short span of a life, whether they are having a love affair or worshipping God. George Herbert wrote religious poetry, but used the devices and imagery you have already seen in Donne. Here are the first two stanzas of Herbert's poem 'Mortification':

How soon doth man decay!
When clothes are taken from a chest of sweets
To swaddle infants, whose young breath
Scarce knows the way;
Those clouts are little winding sheets,
Which do consigne and send them unto death.

When boyes go first to bed,
They step into their voluntarie graves,
Sleep bindes them fast; onely their breath
Makes them not dead:
Successive nights, like rolling waves,
Convey them quickly, who are bound for death.

Knowledge and understanding of the poem (AO2i). This poem carries a traditionally Christian theme, that even in life man faces death. So man should see all of life as a preparation for death, so that he may safely go to heaven on his death.

How the poet expresses meaning (AO3). In the first stanza, Herbert takes the image of a baby wrapped tightly in his first shawls, but says these shawls are like the sheets people are wrapped in when they have died. Babies, even at birth, have an image of death about them. The image is shocking: sweet baby clothes become the clothing of death.

The poem opens with an exclamation that makes the point of the poem clear. Line lengths vary to convey Herbert's message; the short fourth line captures the sense of a baby, innocent and knowing nothing, as yet a very little life. The image is enforced by the rhyme – for example, 'sweets'/'sheets' and 'breath'/'death'. The rhythm varies to follow the movement of the thought.

ACTIVITY 5

Analyse the argument and the language of the second verse of Herbert's poem.

The sonnet form

The sonnet is a short and tightly constructed form of poem, and as such is one of the most difficult forms of poetry to handle.

Much early Elizabethan poetry was in the form of lyrics or sonnets, influenced by the Italian poetry of **Petrarch**. This type of sonnet was written in a specific way, with a division into two parts – the **octet** (first eight lines) and the **sestet** (second six lines). Milton used this form in his Sonnet XIX, 'On His Blindness' (subsequently, this form was often known as the **Miltonic** sonnet):

When I consider how my light is spent,
    Ere half my days, in this dark world and wide,
    And that one talent which is death to hide
    Lodged with me useless, though my soul more bent
To serve therewith my Maker, and present
    My true account, lest he returning chide,
    'Doth God exact day-labor, light denied?'
    I fondly ask. But Patience, to prevent

> *Octet*

That murmur, soon replies: 'God doth not need
    Either man's work or his own gifts; who best
    Bears his mild yoke, they serve him best. His state
Is kingly: thousands at his bidding speed,
    And post o'er land and ocean without rest;
    They also serve who only stand and wait.'

> *Sestet*

(The idea of hiding talents is biblical, relating to the parable in Matthew 25 about using or abusing natural gifts.) How do you analyse this sonnet?

Knowledge and understanding of the poem (AO2i). This is clearly a very personal sonnet. Milton, a devout Puritan, is trying to come to terms with his blindness, and with the thought that this may stop him writing poetry and serving God with his poetic talent. He expresses this anxiety in the octet, the first eight lines, and finds his solution in the sestet. In this last six lines, he argues to himself that he must be patient, that he must accept God's will. By being passive he can serve God as well as can other, more active, people.

How the writer expresses meaning (AO3). Milton's language echoes his themes. In the first two lines there is the contrast between light and dark, physically seeing and not seeing, understanding and not understanding. He uses an image from the Bible to show how his eyesight is used up, or spent, echoing the parable of the spent talents in the gospel of St Matthew, as you have seen. The register, the nature of the language of the whole poem, is religious. Milton wrote the poem to show himself coming to terms with his blindness. He works through his anxiety to a point of acceptance, so that his distress in the early part of the poem seems foolish or 'fond' by the end.

The sestet shows how Milton reasons himself into peace. He personifies the quality of Patience, and by giving it human characteristics sets up an answer, in dialogue, to his first question. This use of dialogue is intended to give the poem a dramatic feel. Again, Milton uses word-play in the word 'best'; he uses 'best' in relation to coming to terms with his blindness as patiently as possible. But the word also applies to finding a new way of serving God through this patience; both ideas are brought together in the word. In a way, the words spoken by Patience are therefore a dramatisation of Milton's inner thoughts and feelings towards his God and his blindness.

You need to work out how, by careful use of language, Milton has been able to say so much in such a short, tight poetic form. Of course, the rhyme helps here. This type of sonnet, the Petrarchan or Miltonic, always uses the same type of rhyme scheme. Notice that in the octet there are two sets of rhymes, based on 'spent' and 'wide'; this keeps the ideas of the octet compact. In the sestet he introduces three different sets of rhymes, based on 'need', 'best' and 'state'. There is extra meaning to be gained when the rhymed words are put together. 'Wide' and 'hide', for example, help to show how Milton cannot face the devastating effects of his blindness, cannot face the world or himself or God. In the sestet, 'state' reminds us of the power of God, whilst 'wait' reminds us of how Milton may best serve him.

ACTIVITY 6

Look at the other rhyming words in Sonnet XIX and see how they bring out the meaning of the poem when they are linked together. For example, consider the impact of the rhymed words 'wide'/'hide'/'chide'/'denied': how do these rhymes support the train of Milton's thought? Similarly, look at 'best'/'rest' and 'state'/'wait'.

Shakespeare used a different form when he wrote his sonnets at the end of the sixteenth century. Here is an example, Sonnet 12:

When I do count the clock that tells the time,
And see the brave day sunk in hideous night;
When I behold the violet past prime,
And sable curls all silver'd o'er with white;
When lofty trees I see barren of leaves,
Which erst from heat did canopy the herd,
And summer's green all girded up in sheaves
Borne on the bier with white and bristly beard;
Then of thy beauty do I question make
That thou among the wastes of time must go,
Since sweets and beauties do themselves forsake,
And die as fast as they see others grow;
And nothing 'gainst Time's scythe can make defence
Save breed, to brave him when he takes thee hence.

Knowledge and understanding of the poem (AO2i). In this sonnet, Shakespeare is concerned with two of his central ideas: the problem of coming to terms with time which is seen to conquer all, and the problem of establishing a love relationship.

How the writer expresses meaning (AO3): Shakespeare doesn't use the same form of the sonnet as Milton. Instead of the octet plus sestet principle of construction, the **Shakespearean Sonnet** uses three four-line sets called **quatrains,** each developing an idea, and a final **couplet** (pair of lines) that poses a solution to these earlier ideas.

In the first quatrain, Shakespeare explains the problem: time does not stand still, night overtakes day just as hair goes grey, and violets go past their best.

The language enhances the theme: the word 'hideous' is strong, and reveals the poet's attitude to time and to death. Shakespeare prepares us for the link into the next quatrain with the words 'violet' and 'sable'; these lines could refer to human beings or to nature; violet eyes or a flower; black hair or an animal. This is really clever, because a sable (which here means an antelope) is renowned for its speed, just like time.

In the next quatrain, Shakespeare looks to nature for examples: trees lose their leaves, and the green crop becomes dried wheat to be used for decorating coffins. Here the ideas of human and animal life are brought together: the dead green crop joins the coffin of the dead human. To human and to natural things, death is inevitable.

The use of **iambic pentameter** supports the meaning. This metre uses a line of five 'feet', each composed of a weakly stressed syllable followed by a heavily stressed one. For example, the sonnet's first line:

> When I do count the clock that tells the time,

You can see that the stressed words predict the whole theme of the poem: *I . . . count . . . clock . . . tells . . . time.* The rhyme scheme also supports the meaning; for example, look at the force of 'time' and 'prime' together. Here we have the whole idea of the poem in a nutshell.

ACTIVITY 7

Using the model developed for the rest of the sonnet, analyse the third quatrain, lines 9–12; then look at how Shakespeare uses the final couplet to resolve the questions he raises within the earlier part of his sonnet.

Wordsworth used the Miltonic sonnet form in his poem 'Composed upon London Bridge':

Earth has not anything to show more fair:
Dull would he be of soul who could pass by
A sight so touching in its majesty:
This City now doth like a garment wear
The beauty of the morning; silent, bare,
Ships, towers, domes, theatres, and temples lie

Open unto the fields, and to the sky;
All bright and glittering in the smokeless air.
Never did sun more beautifully steep
In his first splendour, valley, rock, or hill;
Ne'er saw I, never felt, a calm so deep!
The river glideth at his own sweet will:
Dear God! the very houses seem asleep;
And all that mighty heart is lying still

Knowledge and understanding of the poem (AO2i). In the first eight lines, the octet, Wordsworth describes the beauty of the scene that he is looking at. In the sestet, he moves inward to describe his own responses to the scene and his own feelings.

ACTIVITY 8

Analyse in detail the linked thoughts within the octet and the sestet. Then consider the ways in which Wordsworth expresses these ideas. You should consider: his use of language, including the adjectives and adverbs; his use of alliteration and sibilance, exploring why these are effective; the punctuation and the effect this has on you as you read the sonnet; and the rhythm and rhyme, commenting on why these are effective.

It is now time to turn to a female sonnet writer. Elizabeth Barrett Browning wrote a series of 'Sonnets from the Portuguese'. Robert Browning called Elizabeth his 'Portuguese girl' when he wrote love poems to her, a secret code. So she returned the favour with this sequence. Here is one of her sonnets, 'If Thou Must Love Me . . . ':

If thou must love me, let it be for nought
    Except for love's sake only. Do not say,
    'I love her for her smile – her look – her way
Of speaking gently – for a trick of thought
That falls in well with mine, and certes brought
    A sense of pleasant ease on such a day' –
    For these things in themselves, Beloved, may
Be changed, or change for thee, – and love, so wrought,
May be unwrought so. Neither love me for
    Thine own dear pity's wiping my cheeks dry, –
A creature might forget to weep, who bore
    Thy comfort long, and lose thy love thereby!
But love me for love's sake, that evermore
    Thou may'st love on, through love's eternity.

Knowledge and understanding of the poem (AO2i). As with Shakespeare, you see here a poet concerned about the passing of time and the effect this has on the love between the writer and her loved one. How can they make sure that the love will last?

How the writer expresses meaning (AO3). The form of Elizabeth Barrett Browning's sonnet is loosely Shakespearean, in that it develops four ideas with a conclusion in the final couplet. The thoughts are not as tightly argued or as self-contained as in Shakespeare's sonnets. These sonnets have a relaxed and rather playful feel, so this loosening-up works well.

Her use of dialogue creates a dramatic feeling, as the poet puts herself in her lover's shoes and imagines what he loves about her. This is quite teasing, because Elizabeth Barrett Browning is actually pointing out and praising her own good points, such as her smile, her looks, her voice. She warns him gently not to love her because it just happens to suit him, because things could change one day; so in the conclusion she asks him just to love her fully and uncritically, because only that sort of love will last.

The sonnet is brought to life by the dialogue and its associated punctuation, such as the dashes that control the pace of the poem. The rhymes are regular, again bringing together related words, except for the last: 'eternity' is not full rhyme but an incomplete form known as half rhyme. In this case, the words rhyme on sound. By breaking the pattern of the other full rhymes, the writer makes the word 'eternity', and therefore the meaning of the poem, stand out. The full rhymes used elsewhere suggest the perfection of the love between the two people. The language is gentle and affectionate: 'creature' suggests gentleness, the lover is 'Beloved', and the woman speaks 'gently'. This is a gentle and delicate poem.

Here is another sonnet by Elizabeth Barrett Browning.

Say over again, and yet once over again,
That thou dost love me. Though the word repeated
Should seem a 'cuckoo-song', as thou dost treat it,
Remember, never to the hill or plain,
Valley and wood, without her cuckoo-strain
Comes the fresh Spring in all her green completed.
Beloved, I, amid the darkness greeted
By a doubtful spirit-voice, in that doubt's pain
Cry, 'Speak once more – thou lovest!' Who can fear
Too many stars, though each in heaven shall roll,
Too many flowers, though each shall crown the year?
Say thou dost love me, love me, love me – toll
The silver iterance! – only minding, Dear,
To love me also in silence with thy soul.

ACTIVITY 9

Analyse the ideas of this second poem, and the ways in which Elizabeth Barrett Browning expresses these ideas. You should: trace the sequence of the poet's thoughts; consider the use of dialogue; examine the use of repetition in the language, and how it develops the ideas of the poem ('iterance' means repetition); and consider the tone of the poem.

Narrative poetry

All poetry writers tell a sort of story, often about themselves. In narrative poetry, the poet sets out specifically to tell a tale or to narrate a story to the reader.

Tennyson wrote a lot of narrative poetry, including long poems such as *Maud*. Tennyson called this poem a monodrama because there is just one speaker. One question to ask about narrative poetry is 'How does it hold the reader's interest?' There are two principal answers: the content of the story itself, and variations in the style in which the story is told.

Maud tells of the life and loves of the narrator, who goes through a series of extreme changes of mind and mood in the poem. At first he is mad because of a series of dire family events; then he falls in love with Maud and is happy; then he loses her and is sad and mad again; then he finds consolation in the love of his country.

All these changes are accompanied by different effects in the poetry, differences in the ways in which Tennyson uses language and structure, so language and sound effects change throughout the poem. Here is an extract from the very beginning, where the narrator is distraught about the evil things that have happened to his family:

I hate the dreadful hollow behind the little wood,
Its lips in the field above are dabbled with blood-red heath,
The red-ribb'd ledges drip with a silent horror of blood,
And Echo there, whatever is ask'd her, answers 'Death'.

Knowledge and understanding of the poem (AO2i). This is a very dramatic opening to a poem. We realise that the man is deeply disturbed, and that a murder (that of his father, we find out later), has been committed.

How the writer expresses meaning (AO3). How does Tennyson use language to present the character of the narrator? We realise immediately that the narrator is speaking to the reader; 'I' is the first word. The language, with so many words linked together, creates a build-up of the horror of events: 'hate', 'dreadful', 'blood', 'death'. All the words are linked to the idea of violent bloodshed, but Tennyson does more than this and lets the speaker's words suggest further images. Unbalanced, the speaker personifies the woods as a party to the murder, an animal whose lips are covered with the blood of its prey. The heath, the countryside around, is covered in blood.

Then Tennyson goes on to personify Echo and creates dialogue to support this device. Echo is asked a question, and she tells us all that death has occurred. Tennyson also uses the senses to create this vivid picture – those of sight in the countryside, and taste with the bloody lips, and the sound of the echo, as everyone else is dead.

Here is a later stanza:

> But now shine on, and what care I,
> Who in this stormy gulf have found a pearl
> The countercharm of space and hollow sky,
> And do accept my madness, and would die
> To save from some slight shame one simple girl.

ACTIVITY 10

Analyse the effects that Tennyson creates in this stanza. You should consider: the attitude and ideas of the narrator, with his change of mood; the use of imagery, such as the pearl; the use of language, including the effects created by **alliteration** and **sibilance**; and the effectiveness of the rhythm and rhyme scheme.

John Milton's *Paradise Lost*

Milton faced the same problem of holding an audience's interest when he wrote his epic narrative poem *Paradise Lost*. He resolved this in much the same way as Tennyson did later, by changing the mood and the tone of the poem repeatedly, and by using language techniques just as subtle as those of Tennyson.

Knowledge and understanding of the poem (AO2i). Milton, a devout Christian, wrote his long poem to explain how it was that because man disobeyed God by eating the apple to gain more knowledge than he should, he lost Paradise and was forced to live a harder life in a crueller world. Milton uses many different language techniques to hold the reader's interest because he had another problem: his story was not new. Most readers of his time, and even in our own time, knew the story of Adam and Eve.

How the writer expresses these ideas (AO3). Here are some of the techniques Milton used to keep the reader interested.

(1) *He divides the poem up*: there are twelve 'books', each telling the story from a different perspective at different stages as events develop.
(2) *The location of the books varies* – heaven, hell, paradise, and the new world of Adam and Eve.
(3) *Milton varies the narrator* in the books as different speakers pick up the thread of the poem. God and his son speak, angels tell the story, devils in hell

speak; Satan narrates, Adam and Eve explain their viewpoints. The language changes with the different speakers. Here are some words spoken by God:

'[. . .] In mercy and justice both,
Through heav'n and earth, so shall my glory excel,
But mercy first and last shall brightest shine.'

The language gives us an account of the nature of God. All the words speak of goodness – 'mercy', 'justice', 'glory'. We know that God is all-powerful through the use of the word 'my'.
(4) *The rhythm of the poem uses iambic pentameter*, a line with five heavy stresses that you have already seen in Shakespeare's Sonnet 12. Elsewhere in the poem, Milton uses this metre to suggest anger or distress, but here the lines flow easily to suggest ease and harmony:

Through heav'n and earth, so shall my glory excel,

Notice that the stress falls on key words or parts of words to enforce Milton's meaning: *heav'n . . . earth . . . shall . . . glory . . . excel*. In this way, Milton hammers home to the reader the main point of his line; as you can see, the iambic pentameter is essential here.
(5) *The word order is significant*, with important words coming at the ends of the lines: 'both', 'excel', 'shine'.

Now look at this next extract from *Paradise Lost*. Here, Beelzebub is speaking to the devils:

'[. . .] And what peace can we return,
But to our power hostility and hate,
Untamed reluctance, and revenge though slow,
Yet ever plotting how the Conqueror least
May reap his conquest, and may least rejoice
In doing what we most in suffering feel?
[. . .]'

ACTIVITY 11

Analyse Beelzebub's speech and then compare it to the language of God in the earlier extract. Here are some approaches you could take. Start by looking at the register of the language – that of war – and decide how this is suggested. What is the tone? How does Beelzebub refer to God, and what does this tell us of his attitude? Try to work out the underlying feelings of Beelzebub and the other devils. Why does Beelzebub ask a question? Consider how the rhythm works to stress certain words.

(5) *The use of dialogue breaks up the narrative*, as you have just seen, to give dramatic variation, and changes of tone and pace.

(6) *Milton also changes the tone of the poetry*. At times it has terrific dramatic force, as when we see Satan take flight:

> Forthwith upright he rears from off the pool
> His mighty stature; on each hand the flames
> Driv'n backward slope their pointing spires, and rolled
> In billows, leave i' th' midst a horrid vale.

Such powerful words are used to create a picture; we see Satan's huge size, his power as he takes flight; he carries images of the fire of Hell, trailing long flames behind him.

Milton controls the language to suggest the speed of Satan's flight: he abbreviates words in the fourth line of the extract; and he breaks the second line with a pause to suggest Satan poising himself to take off. Nature as we know it is reversed so that the 'billows' of the sea become flames, and the peaceful valley becomes evil. Why? Because Milton is giving us a sense of the power of Satan. Remember that Satan is out to destroy Adam and Eve, and we are bound to think that they do not have much of a chance.

In complete contrast, Book Nine contains a picture of Eve through Satan's eyes. The tone and mood change completely, giving rise to a passage of beautiful lyrical poetry:

> . . . Eve separate he spies,
> Veiled in a cloud of fragrance, where she stood,
> Half spied, so thick the roses bushing round
> About her glowed, oft stooping to support
> Each flow'r of slender stalk, whose head though gay
> Carnation, purple, azure, or specked with gold,
> Hung drooping unsustained; . . .

Here the language is very **sensuous**, which means that it draws on the senses – in this case, of sight, smell and touch ('**sensual**' means related to sexuality). Milton uses sibilance (letters like 's' with a soft hissing sound, truly the sound of a snake hissing) and alliteration (a sequence of words beginning with the same sound, such as 's' again).

ACTIVITY 9

Analyse the ways in which Milton achieves his effects in this description of Eve. You should think about: the use of the senses; the way the flowers are described, and how Eve is placed amongst them; the use of punctuation and its effect on rhythm and meaning; and the use of consonants to create sound effects.

Remember that this picture is seen through Satan's eyes. There is great sadness and irony: we appreciate the simplicity, beauty and frailty of the human Eve, and the peace and happiness she is about to lose.

These in essence are the central characteristics of Milton's verse. He sets descriptions of character against character, and situation against situation. (For example, the later picture of Adam and Eve when they confront God and each other is a total contrast to what Satan saw originally.) He sets descriptions of places against each other. And he varies mood and tone and the stresses on words within the iambic pentameter line.

The whole of *Paradise Lost* is a tapestry of different effects, with Milton intervening with a lyrical prayer dedicating his work to God:

Hail, holy Light, offspring of Heav'n first-born,
Or of th' Eternal coeternal beam
May I express thee unblamed? . . .

There is one point of conflict about Milton's poem that you should consider. Satan's descriptions, events seen through his eyes such as the beautiful picture of Eve, are powerful and seductive to the reader. In a way, our sympathies are often drawn to this attractive anti-hero. Did Milton do this to make you feel the powerful attraction of evil, which finally defeated Adam and Eve? Or was it a misjudgement on Milton's part; did he make the evil characters too attractive? What do you think?

Aspects of the poetry of Chaucer

If you study Chaucer's poetry, you will probably turn to *The Canterbury Tales*, a series of stories told by pilgrims on their way from London to Canterbury. These tales were written towards the end of the fourteenth century, which means that they are medieval literature. So you should begin by looking at how medieval influences affected the ideas in the *Tales* and the ways in which they were written.

Knowledge and understanding of the poem (AO2i). Some of the ideas behind Chaucer's poetry are derived from a form known as the Romance, which reflected the nature of medieval society. There were two clear codes of conduct for a knight in medieval times: **Courtly Love** (or the Love Religion), which laid down rules for a knight wishing to 'court' a woman, and the **Chivalric Code**, which decreed how a knight should behave on and off the battlefield.

According to the traditions of Courtly Love, a knight must worship his lady, who must be remote, mysterious, aloof and chaste. There must be no sexual conquest until a large number of rituals have been performed. These ideas were drawn from French literature, notably *The Romance of the Rose* which explored the spiritual aspects of love. According to the Chivalric Code, the knight at the same time owes duties of loyalty and brotherly love to his leader and his fellow knights. This loyalty is sacred and unbreakable. The result was that a knight was subject to two sets of rules, one of love and one of war, which often caused conflicts of loyalty and behaviour. This and other sorts of conflict lie at the heart of *The Canterbury Tales*, which Chaucer uses to explore contradictions and difficulties within medieval society.

Conflict appears throughout the *Tales*. In *The Wife of Bath's Tale* and its Prologue, Chaucer presents the conflicts between the 'experience' of the Wife and the heartless teachings of the church, led by dry old men; he also explores the conflict between a woman's point of view generally, and the point of view of the anti-female clerics or church officers. In *The Merchant's Tale,* Chaucer mocks the courtly love tradition. Januarie, an old man, is almost a parody of the courtly knight pursuing a lady; and his young wife is herself a mockery of the chaste courtly lady. In this poem Chaucer refers to the tradition of Courtly Love and *The Romance of the Rose*. In *The Pardoner's Tale*, Chaucer explores the conflicts that occur when the rules of chivalric behaviour are thrown aside.

ACTIVITY 13

Look through your text and pick out the different conflicts that occur. Decide whether any of these are related to either of the two codes of conduct. Is Chaucer saying that it is impossible to obey both, or perhaps that it is foolish to ignore them? Or is he suggesting that the two codes are now out of date?

How the writer expresses meaning (AO3).
(1) *Structure.* The medieval influence on *The Canterbury Tales* is not just restricted to the ideas but also extends to the structure. There is a different sort of method of construction at work here. In modern times we tend to expect a logical and clearly sequenced piece of literature. But the medieval mind did not work like this. Think of an old cathedral like Durham or Wells or Winchester – perhaps you could look at a picture of one. The building is a mass of different styles: outside there will be those curving, supporting arches known as flying buttresses next to intricate carved statues; inside there may be a real mishmash of styles. There will be intricate little statues in niches again, and large statues, delicate filigree designs on the plaster of the walls, and huge soaring plain arches. All the component parts will be different, but the overall effect is of a beautiful and majestic building.

ACTIVITY 14

Look at the photographs of the inside and outside of Salisbury Cathedral, and note the different styles that you see.

The approach of the medieval cathedral builders mirrors the way Chaucer constructed his poetry – a combination of different styles; movements in time that go backwards and forwards; contradictions; mixtures of language from the homely and colloquial to formal literary language, ambiguity and irony; and the use of '**digressions**' – a key word in Chaucer. All these elements are **interlaced** to give the final tapestry effect of the poem's form and structure.

Chaucer's use of language

(2) *Irony* is important in a discussion of Chaucer's work; it is a sophisticated form of sarcasm, where the real meaning of a phrase is disguised behind another. Chaucer is quite wicked in mocking his characters. See how he introduces the Merchant in the *General Prologue*: a 'forked beard', dressed 'In mottley'. A forked beard? Does this suggest that he is confused in his ideas? Does motley clothing suggest that he is a bit of a mess in terms of fashion and ideas? Worst of all, Chaucer calls him 'worthy' – a word always used ironically: he is suggesting that the Merchant is vain, self-important and dim. Similarly, the knight is called worthy, when he in fact betrays all the knightly ideals.

Chaucer develops all these qualities with irony in the tale itself. The Merchant's name is ironical. 'Januarie' is an old man in the winter of his life – does he have the right to choose a beautiful young wife? 'He atte laste appointed himself on oon'. He was absolutely blind to these mistakes as Chaucer makes clear: 'For love is blind alday, and may not see'. The Merchant excitedly takes his beautiful young wife to bed, but he is unaware of what he looks like to a young woman. Chaucer gives us her point of view when he intrudes into the tale to describe the old man:

The slakke skyn aboute his nekke shaketh,
Whil that he sang, so chaunteth he and craketh.
But God woot what that May thoughte in hir herte,
Whan she hym saugh up sittynge in his sherte,
In his nyght-cappe, and with his nekke lene;
She preyseth nat his pleyyng worth a bene.

ACTIVITY 15

Look at the times when we see the old man through May's eyes, and decide what sort of image this presents to you. Why do you think that Chaucer creates this viewpoint? Could it be to suggest that Januarie is wrong to seek a young wife? is it to make you feel sympathetic towards May?

(3) *Imagery*. As in any poetry, the imagery that Chaucer uses supports the meaning of the poem. In *The Wife of Bath's Tale*, there is much imagery related to animals, usually about the wife herself. In *The Pardoner's Tale*, there are references to money throughout, which suits the character of the money-grabbing hypocrite of a showman. In *The Knight's Tale*, there are constant images referring to God.

The imagery in *The Merchant's Tale* is very important. It often relates to nature such as the weather or the seasons, as this suggests the idea of the old merchant and his young wife – Januarie is in the winter of his life, and May is in the spring or summer of hers. In lines 1319 and 1702, he refers to marriage as a sacrament; throughout the Tale the merchant uses a religious register or religious images. This is important, and allows Chaucer to create some sympathy for the old man.

The merchant seems to reveal a genuine love for May when he says:

'Rys up, my wyf, my love, my lady free!
The turtles voys is herd, my dowve sweete; . . .
Thou hast me wounded in myn herte, O wyf!
No spot of thee ne knew I al my lif.

The animal imagery of the turtle and the dove compares May to these gentle creatures, who traditionally represent love. Januarie seems genuinely distressed, and Chaucer manipulates the reader's sympathy towards the old man, who goes on to admit his faults and his jealousy.

Cleverly, Chaucer had kept May quiet throughout the poem for almost 2000 words. When she speaks, this confirms an impression you may have of a heartless young woman who takes advantage of an old man. Far from being demure, she is loud and hypocritical, assuring Januarie that she too has 'a soule for to kepe'. She is indeed 'fresh' in being quick-thinking and lusty, and as quick-witted as the Wife of Bath.

This creates the great irony within the poem in the blindness/sight sequence. It is Januarie's blindness that enables him to see the true nature of his wife.

ACTIVITY 16

Make a list of the ironies you find in the Tale that you are studying. Try to work out why Chaucer creates these ironies, and the effect they have upon you.

(4) There are other matters of *style* that you need to consider when reading any of the Tales. You should look at the puns, the use of scholarly language and of exaggerations; and spoken words that ironically do not always suit the speaker. All are part of Chaucer's 'interlacing' effect.

(5) *Digressions* matter in Chaucer's writing. They occur when Chaucer or the storyteller seems to ramble off the point; but like the embroidery around a medieval tapestry they embroider and illustrate the ideas of the Tale. *The Wife of Bath*, for example, frequently interrupts her argument to digress – look at line 323, when she seems to drift off to talk about Ptolemy, and line 951, when she talks about Midas. But if you think about these so-called digressions, you see that both say something about male–female relationships that has not yet been said in the poem.

In *The Merchant's Tale*, there appear to be digressions in the episodes between Pluto and Proserpina; but these are used to frame the actions that we see in the human aspects of the Tale – in a way, their ideas represent the inner impulses of Januarie and May.

In Chaucer's poetry there are two movements: there is the forward movement of the tale itself; and there are sideways movements to elaborate upon various points, as in the 'digressions'. Again, this is part of Chaucer's 'interlacing' effect.

(6) Chaucer often uses *proverbs* to prove his points, and in so doing provides a contrast to the biblical or scholarly language that he normally uses. Frequently, to make sure that we do not miss a point, Chaucer drops the pretence of the speaker's voice and intervenes in the poem himself. You saw him do this in the lines above from *The Merchant's Tale*, where he intruded with a homely saying or aphorism and told us, the readers, that love was always blind. This is a saying we still use today.

(7) The form of the *General Prologue* and many other parts of the Tales is that of the **heroic couplet** – iambic pentameters rhymed in pairs. (See page 61 above to remind yourself about iambic pentameters.) Here is another example:

> . . . she saugh, wher Damyan
> Sat in the bussh, and coughen she bigan,
> And with hir fynger signes made she
> That Damyan sholde clymbe upon a tree.

ACTIVITY 17

Work out the effects of Chaucer's use of heroic couplets in this extract, and the effect of the rhyme in bringing certain words together. How does the metre help to convey meaning? What do you learn of the character of May and of Damyan here?

ACTIVITY 18

Make a list of those aspects or characteristics of Chaucer's style that you now know. Find examples of each, and work out how these different devices are effective in conveying the ideas within the Tale that you are studying.

This completes the work on poetry and the two related Assessment Objectives for the first section of AS Module 2. You are well on the way towards gaining 'knowledge and understanding' of poetry, and of the ways in which poets' 'choices of form, structure and language shape meanings'.

Preparing for the examination

This module uses a closed book examination, so you will not be able to take your texts in with you. But don't worry: where appropriate, the paper includes the full texts of shorter poems or extracts from longer poems.

Section B: Drama

In this section you are tested on three Assessment Objectives. Look back at the table on page 49 to see how the 40 (that is, 20 doubled) marks for this section are allocated. You can see that the key Assessment Objective for the drama section is AO5i, 'show understanding of the contexts in which literary texts are written and understood'.

At AS Level, you're concerned with the contexts that are apparent in your reading of the text, and how these contexts affect the way you think about it. This is the focus of the examination questions, so it's important that you try to identify contexts as you read the play, and then explore how they appear and what they add to your understanding of the play's purposes and meanings. Most of this section is therefore devoted to an exploration of some of the different types of contexts that you might find in the plays you're studying.

Part-to-whole contexts

In many ways this is the simplest context to think about – it means relating an extract or a part of the text to the rest of the text, showing its importance or significance. You may well have looked at parts of texts in similar ways in your GCSE course. There are a number of elements to consider, though, if you're going to tackle this successfully.

Here's an example from Arthur Miller's *Death of a Salesman*:

WILLY: [*astonished*]: What're you doing? What're you doing? [to LINDA] Why is he crying?

BIFF: [*crying, broken*]: Will you let me go, for Christ's sake? Will you take that phony dream and burn it before something happens? [*Struggling to contain himself, he pulls away and moves to the stairs.*] I'll go in the morning. Put him – put him to bed. [*Exhausted,* BIFF *moves up the stairs to his room.*]

WILLY: [*after a long pause, astonished, elevated*]: Isn't that – isn't that remarkable? Biff – he likes me!

LINDA: He loves you, Willy!

HAPPY: [*deeply moved*]: Always did, Pop.

WILLY: Oh, Biff! [*Staring wildly*] He cried! Cried to me. [*He is choking with his love, and now cries out his promise*] That boy – that boy is going to be magnificent!

[BEN *appears in the light just outside the kitchen.*]

BEN: Yes, outstanding, with twenty thousand behind him.

LINDA: [*sensing the racing of his mind, fearfully, carefully*]: Now come to bed, Willy. It's all settled now.

WILLY: [*Finding it difficult not to rush out of the house*]: Yes, we'll sleep. Come on. Go to sleep, Hap.

BEN: And it does take a great kind of a man to crack the jungle.

[*In accents of dread,* BEN's *idyllic music starts up.*]

HAPPY: [*his arm around* LINDA]: I'm getting married, Pop, don't forget it. I'm changing everything. I'm gonna run that department before the year is up. You'll see, Mom. [*He kisses her.*]

BEN: The jungle is dark but full of diamonds, Willy.

[WILLY *turns, moves, listening to* BEN.]

LINDA: Be good. You're both good boys, just act that way, that's all.

HAPPY: 'Night, Pop. [*He goes upstairs.*]

LINDA: [*to* WILLY]: Come, dear.

BEN: [*with greater force*]: One must go in to fetch a diamond out.

There are several things in this extract that have a bearing on the rest of the play. For example, when Biff refers to 'that phony dream', he's referring to Willy's impossible dream of what Biff might become. But here the context of the American Dream (see below) is clearly in Miller's mind, and the audience's; it informs all of Willy's hopes and actions, and is the criterion against which many of the other characters' words and actions are measured.

Willy's 'he likes me' comes out of nowhere, with little evidence in the text that he should think so here. Perhaps it's the beginning of the fantasy that is about to overwhelm him. Whether it is or not, the drive to be liked is important to him throughout the play, and he wants this for his sons too – it's one of his measures of success.

'That boy – that boy is going to be magnificent!' is echoed many times in the play, as an expression of Willy's hopes for his sons. Here, it has a tragic ring about it – Biff has just shown himself to be the opposite of magnificent, and not appropriate to Willy's dream. Willy is clearly deluded in some way.

The stage directions here recall their use throughout the play. Ben appears in a different light to that used for the rest of the stage, which is how lighting is used to suggest Willy's visions. Ben's music appears, too – but here it is referred to as 'idyllic', as Ben represents Willy's ideal. It has 'accents of dread', though, for the only time, suggesting the tragedy to come. Ben is real to Willy, he 'turns, moves, listening to Ben'. This is at the heart of the tragedy of the play, too: Ben represents the success that Willy can never attain, and listening to him here brings on Willy's fatal decision.

Ben's words 'the jungle is dark but full of diamonds' refer to his reported success earlier in the play, which Willy has always taken as a perfect example. 'The jungle' suggests danger, and the jungle of competition. There's threat here, and Ben's repetition – 'one must go in to fetch a diamond out' – said 'with greater force', underlines an urgency to act, perhaps desperately, to achieve something. This is what Willy does, tragically.

Happy's words here cannot now be believed, especially after Willy's remarks about Biff. The audience can only see Happy as 'a chip off the old block' – a man with all of Willy's values, lies and self-delusion. His words are echoes of Willy elsewhere in the play.

The next extract from *Death of a Salesman* is the opening of Act Two. Again, try to work out how it relates to the rest of the play:

Music is heard, gay and bright. The curtain rises as the music fades away.
[WILLY, *in shirt sleeves, is sitting at the kitchen table, sipping coffee, his hat in his lap.* LINDA *is filling his cup when she can.*]

WILLY: Wonderful coffee. Meal in itself.

LINDA: Can I make you some eggs?

WILLY: No. Take a breath.

LINDA: You look so rested, dear.

WILLY: I slept like a dead one. First time in months. Imagine, sleeping till ten on a Tuesday morning. Boys left nice and early, heh?

LINDA: They were out of here by eight o'clock.

WILLY: Good work!

LINDA: It was so thrilling to see them leaving together. I can't get over the shaving lotion in this house!

WILLY: [*smiling*]: Mmm –

LINDA: Biff was very changed this morning. His whole attitude seemed to be hopeful. He couldn't wait to get downtown to see Oliver.

WILLY: He's heading for a change. There's no question, there simply are certain men that take longer to get solidified. How did he dress?

LINDA: His blue suit. He's so handsome in that suit. He could be a – anything in that suit!
[WILLY *gets up from the table.* LINDA *holds his jacket for him.*]

WILLY: There's no question, no question at all. Gee, on the way home tonight I'd like to buy some seeds.

LINDA: [*laughing*]: That'd be wonderful. But not enough sun gets back there. Nothing'll grow any more.

WILLY: You wait, kid, before it's all over we're gonna get a little place out in the country, and I'll raise some vegetables, a couple of chickens . . .

LINDA: You'll do it yet, dear

ACTIVITY 19

This is an apparently quiet moment in an often highly dramatic play – but there is much here that relates to the rest. Show how this extract relates to the rest of the play by answering these questions:

- Think about the effect of the music here. The audience has already heard music extensively in Act One, so is alive to its significance. Coming at the beginning of Act Two, what might it suggest here?

- Everything seems to be going well here. List the things in the extract that contribute to this perception, and consider what happens later in the play. These things are highlighted, of course, by their position in the structure – they're an opening impression for the second half of the play.

- Consider the effect of these phrases in the context of the rest of the play: 'I slept like a dead one'; 'He's heading for a change' (about Biff); 'You'll do it yet'.

- Trace the idea of being 'solidified' in the play. Willy uses it several times as praise, whereas Biff feels 'temporary' about himself, and wants a 'steady' girl, with 'substance'. Look at where and when it's used, and think about it in relation to the meanings of the play.

- Willy is in optimistic mood and wants to buy seeds – again, a common occurrence in the play – but the sun is blocked by the building. What does all this imply? Look for the last time this is referred to, and what it means for Willy and those watching him.

It's useful to practise this skill with key scenes from the play you're studying. Broadly, you should be looking for ideas in the scene that are reflected or developed elsewhere in the play, and contexts that might be significant. Features of language are important, and so are stage directions. Any indications of music, sound, lights, costume and on-stage action could be significant.

Socio-economic contexts

Most plays have a social context. They are set in a particular society at a particular time, and have something to say about this context – and this is often related to the economic conditions that apply to that society, or at least to the people within it who are shown on stage.

Here's another extract from *Death of a Salesman*:

HAPPY:	We always told the truth!
BIFF:	[*turning on him*]: You big blow, are you the assistant buyer? You're one of the two assistants to the assistant, aren't you?
HAPPY:	Well, I'm practically –
BIFF:	You're practically full of it! We all are! And I'm through with it. [*To* WILLY] Now hear this, Willy, this is me.
WILLY:	I know you!
BIFF:	You know why I had no address for three months? I stole a suit in Kansas City and I was in jail. [*To* LINDA, *who is sobbing*] Stop crying. I'm through with it.

[LINDA *turns away from them, her hands covering her face.*]

WILLY:	I suppose that's my fault!
BIFF:	I stole myself out of every good job since high school!
WILLY:	And whose fault is that?
BIFF:	And I never got anywhere because you blew me so full of hot air I could never stand taking orders from anybody! That's whose fault it is!
WILLY:	I hear that!
LINDA:	Don't, Biff!
BIFF:	It's goddam time you heard that! I had to be boss big shot in two weeks, and I'm through with it!
WILLY:	Then hang yourself! For spite, hang yourself!
BIFF:	No! Nobody's hanging himself, Willy! I ran down eleven flights with a pen in my hand today. And suddenly I stopped, you hear me? And in the middle of that office building, do you hear this? I stopped in the middle of that building and I saw – the sky. I saw the things that I love in this world. The work and the food and time to sit and smoke. And I looked at the pen and said to myself, what the hell am I grabbing this for? Why am I trying to become what I don't want to be? What am I doing in an office, making a contemptuous, begging fool of myself, when all I want is out there, waiting for me the minute I say I know who I am! Why can't I say that, Willy? [*He tries to make* WILLY *face him, but* WILLY *pulls away and moves to the left.*]
WILLY:	[*with hatred, threateningly*]: The door of your life is wide open!
BIFF:	Pop! I'm a dime a dozen, and so are you!
WILLY:	[*turning on him now in an uncontrolled outburst*]: I am not a dime a dozen! I am Willy Loman, and you are Biff Loman!

[BIFF *starts for* WILLY, *but is blocked by* HAPPY. *In his fury,* BIFF *seems on the verge of attacking his father.*]

BIFF:	I am not a leader of men, Willy, and neither are you. You were never anything but a hard-working drummer who landed in the ash-can like all the rest of

> them! I'm one dollar an hour, Willy! I tried seven states and couldn't raise it. A buck an hour! Do you gather my meaning? I'm not bringing home any prizes any more, and you're going to stop waiting for me to bring them home!
>
> WILLY: [*directly to* BIFF]: You vengeful, spiteful mut!
>
> [BIFF *breaks from* HAPPY. WILLY, *in fright, starts up the stairs.* BIFF *grabs him.*]
>
> BIFF: [*at the peak of his fury*] Pop, I'm nothing! I'm nothing, Pop. Can't you understand that? There's no spite in it any more. I'm just what I am, that's all.
>
> [BIFF's *fury has spent itself and he breaks down, sobbing, holding on to* WILLY, *who dumbly fumbles for* BIFF's *face.*]
>
> WILLY: [*astonished*]: What're you doing? What're you doing? [*To* LINDA] Why is he crying?
>
> BIFF: [*crying, broken*]: Will you let me go, for Christ's sake? Will you take that phony dream and burn it before something happens?

The context here is, essentially, the socio-economic concept of the 'American Dream'. Willy has built his life on the desire to succeed in business, which will bring wealth, respect and happiness, and has instilled this belief in his children. The effect is disastrous – Biff is totally unlike his father, so his attempts to conform to Willy's dreams produce a broken man, as here, whereas Happy is all too like his father, in that he lies to himself and others about what he does and what he is.

Happy is exposed as a liar about his job here. His last speech in the play, a page on from this (see the extract on page 74 above) shows that he has learned nothing from this moment. Willy's 'I know you!' is a delusion – he means that he knows what he believes Biff to be, though the audience knows that Biff isn't what Willy thinks he is. He believes Biff to have a 'magnificent' future as a successful, well liked and wealthy man. He tells him that 'The door of your life is wide open!', by which he means that Biff can still follow in his father's footsteps – or rather the footsteps he would like to have made.

Willy's instilled attitudes have caused Biff to steal to acquire the symbols of success that he can't get any other way, and to gain an inflated view of himself in relation to others – he 'could never stand taking orders from anybody'. Having to be the 'boss' is part of this socio-economic mind set. For Willy, the alternative to success is self-destruction – 'Then hang yourself' – so strongly does he believe in it. This leads us to the end of the play. Willy is literally destroyed by his 'phony dream'.

Miller's critique of the American Dream is not simply economic. It is about what it does to the individual, in that it distorts people's perceptions of their own identity. 'Why am I trying to become what I don't want to be?' pleads Biff, wanting something different, which he thinks will be his when 'I say I know who I am'. Again, Willy's 'I know you!' is not true.

The social truth is that neither Willy nor Biff is a leader of men, and the economic truth is that they are both 'hard-working drummers who landed in the ash-can'. Think of Willy's evident money troubles, throughout the play and by implication before it, and what this leads him to. Willy cannot face this truth, as his dreams have too strong a hold on him – Biff is 'vengeful, spiteful' for telling the truth, and Willy cannot understand why Biff is crying. The destruction of his life's dreams leads him to a fantasy world, which he inhabits throughout the play, and eventually to his own destruction.

Now read one more extract from the same play:

BEN: You've a new continent at your doorstep, William. Get out of these cities, they're full of talk and time payments and courts of law. Screw on your fists and you can fight for a fortune up there.

WILLY: Yes, yes! Linda, Linda!

[LINDA *enters as of old, with the wash.*]

LINDA: Oh, you're back?

BEN: I haven't much time.

WILLY: No, wait! Linda, he's got a proposition for me in Alaska.

LINDA: But you've got – [*To* BEN] He's got a beautiful job here.

WILLY: But in Alaska, kid, I could –

LINDA: You're doing well enough, Willy!

BEN: [*to* LINDA]: Enough for what, my dear?

LINDA: [*frightened of* BEN *and angry at him*]: Don't say those things to him! Enough to be happy right here, right now. [*To* WILLY, *while* BEN *laughs*] Why must everybody conquer the world? You're well liked, and the boys love you, and someday – [*to* BEN] – why, old man Wagner told him just the other day that if he keeps it up he'll be a member of the firm, didn't he, Willy?

WILLY: Sure, sure. I am building something with this firm, Ben, and if a man is building something he must be on the right track, mustn't he?

BEN: What are you building? Lay your hand on it. Where is it?

WILLY: [*hesitantly*]: That's true, Linda, there's nothing.

LINDA: Why? [*to* BEN] There's a man eighty-four years old –

WILLY: That's right, Ben, that's right. When I look at that man I say, what is there to worry about?

BEN: Bah!

WILLY: It's true, Ben. All he has to do is go into any city, pick up the phone, and he's making his living and you know why?

BEN: [*picking up his valise*]: I've got to go.

WILLY: [*holding* BEN *back*]: Look at this boy!

[BIFF, *in his high-school sweater, enters carrying suitcase.* HAPPY *carries* BIFF's *shoulder guards, gold helmet, and football pants.*]

WILLY: Without a penny to his name, three great universities are begging for him, and from there the sky's the limit, because it's not what you do, Ben. It's who you know and the smile on your face! It's contacts, Ben, contacts! The whole wealth of Alaska passes over the lunch table at the Commodore Hotel, and that's the wonder, the wonder of this country, that a man can end with diamonds here on the basis of being liked! [*He turns to* BIFF.] And that's why when you get out on that field today it's important. Because thousands of people will be rooting for you and loving you. [*To* BEN, *who has again begun to leave*] And Ben! when he walks into a business office his name will sound out like a bell and all the doors will open to him! I've seen it, Ben, I've seen it a thousand times! You can't feel it with your hand like timber, but it's there!

BEN: Good-bye, William.

WILLY: Ben, am I right? Don't you think I'm right? I value your advice.

BEN: There's a new continent at your doorstep, William. You could walk out rich. Rich! [*He is gone.*]

WILLY: We'll do it here, Ben! You hear me? We're gonna do it here!

ACTIVITY 20

Explore the socio-economic context revealed in this extract. Here are some points to consider:

- Part of the American Dream lies in the frontier myth of a new, open area to be conquered. How is this reflected here? Consider who says it.

- Why is 'enough' not good enough?

- This is the past, in Willy's head; he's mostly optimistic here. But find and think about moments in the extract when a darker reality is suggested, even in his own words.

- 'The sky's the limit' is a phrase that belongs to this mind set; how is it undermined here? (Think who Willy is referring to when he says it.)

- 'A man can end with diamonds here on the basis of being liked!' Think about the last reference to 'diamonds' (page 74), and what it comes to mean.

- 'We're gonna do it here!' Willy means they're going to be successful and rich and well liked here. That's the Dream – but what is the truth?

Contexts of class and education

Class and education clearly have close connections with social and economic contexts, but they can be looked at separately. Here's an extract from the beginning of Willy Russell's play *Educating Rita*:

RITA: Well, I'm a student now, aren't I? I'll have to do exams, won't I?

FRANK: Yes, eventually.

RITA: I'll have to learn about it all, won' I? Yeh. It's like y' sit there, don't y', watchin' the ballet or the opera on the telly an' – an' y' call it rubbish cos that's what it looks like? Cos y' don't understand. So y' switch it off an' say, that's fuckin' rubbish.

FRANK: Do you?

RITA: I do. But I don't want to. I wanna see. Y' don't mind me swearin', do y'?

FRANK: Not at all.

RITA: Do you swear?

FRANK: Never stop.

RITA: See, the educated classes know it's only words, don't they? It's only the masses who don't understand. I do it to shock them sometimes. Y' know when I'm in the hairdresser's – that's where I work – I'll say somethin' like, 'Oh, I'm really fucked', y' know, dead loud. It doesn't half cause a fuss.

FRANK: Yes – I'm sure . . .

RITA: But it doesn't cause any sort of fuss with educated people, does it? Cos they know it's only words and they don't worry. But these stuck-up idiots I meet, they think they're royalty just cos they don't swear; an' I wouldn't mind but it's the aristocracy that swears more than anyone, isn't it? They're effin' an' blindin' all day long. It's all 'Pass me the fackin' grouse' with them, isn't it? But y' can't tell them that round our way. It's not their fault; they can't help it. [*She goes to the window and looks out.*] But sometimes I hate them. God, what's it like to be free?

In this extract, Rita identifies a number of things that she thinks belong to a higher class than her own. She sees 'the ballet or the opera' as cultural pursuits, though she talks about seeing them 'on the telly'. Later her view is refined – and her reaction to her visit to the theatre, reported in Act I Scene 6, is a significant move.

Rita contrasts the attitude of 'the educated classes' with that of 'the masses'. Although she sees herself as belonging to the 'masses' here, she contrasts their attitude to language with her own. Her attitude to class and education in relation to language is complex. She swears freely – much more than Frank in the play, despite his protestation here. Rita's comments, 'so y' switch it off an' say, that's fuckin' rubbish' reflects not just herself, but how she perceives her class (that's the effect of her use of 'y'). At the same time, she thinks that 'the educated classes know it's only words', and contrast, their attitude to that of the 'stuck-up idiots' she meets, presumably in the hairdresser's. 'They think they're royalty just 'cos they don't swear' suggests that the people she describes think that they belong to a higher class than 'the masses', but in fact they don't.

Through the attitude she expresses to culture, Rita shows that she identifies herself with the masses, but wants to change: 'I do. But I don't want to. I wanna see.' She feels alienated from her class – 'sometimes I hate them' – and longs to change – 'what's it like to be free?' In the context of the passage and the play, we can interpret being 'free' as being educated, and transcending her background.

Now have a look at another extract from *Educating Rita*.

FRANK: Well, look around you.
RITA: I do. But don't see any, *y'* know, culture. I just see everyone pissed, or on the Valium, tryin' to get from one day to the next. Y' daren't say that round our way like, cos they're proud. They'll tell *y'* they've got culture as they sit there drinkin' their keg beer out of plastic glasses.
FRANK: Yes, but there's nothing wrong with that, if they're content with it.
[*During the following* FRANK's *attention is caught gradually and he stops marking and starts listening.*]
RITA: But they're not. Cos there's no meanin'. They tell *y'* stories about the past, *y'* know, the war, or when they were fightin' for food an' clothin' an' houses. Their eyes light up as they tell *y'*, because there was some meanin' to it. But the thing is that now, I mean now that most of them have got some sort of house an' there's food an' money around, they know they're better off but, honest, they know they've got nothin' as well. There's like this sort of disease, but no one mentions it; everyone behaves as though it's normal, *y'* know inevitable that there's vandalism an' violence an' houses burnt out an' wrecked by the people they were built for. There's somethin' wrong. An' like the worst thing is that *y'* know the people who are supposed to like represent the

people on our estate, y' know the *Daily Mirror* an' the *Sun*, an' ITV an' the Unions, what are they tellin' people to do? They just tell them to go out an' get more money, don't they? But they don't want more money; it's like me, isn't it? Y' know, buyin' new dresses all the time, isn't it? The Unions tell them to go out an' get more money an' ITV an' the papers tell them what to spend it on so the disease is always covered up.

[FRANK *swivels round in his chair to face* RITA.]

FRANK: [*after a pause*]: Why didn't you take a course in politics?

RITA: Politics? Go way, I hate politics. I'm just tellin' y' about round our way. I wanna be on this course findin' out. You know what I learn from you, about art an' literature, it feeds me, inside. I can get through the rest of the week if I know I've got comin' here to look forward to. Denny tried to stop me comin' tonight. He tried to get me to go out to the pub with him an' his mates. He hates me comin' here. It's like drug addicts, isn't it? They hate it when one of them tries to break away. It makes me stronger comin' here. That's what Denny's frightened of.

ACTIVITY 21

Find and explore all the references to class and education in the extract, and think how they reflect attitudes and ideas in the rest of the play. Here are ideas and questions to help you.

(1) Think about what Rita means by the word 'culture' in her first line.

(2) What are the elements of the culture of 'the masses' that she mentions here? (Think about drink, drugs, the media, consumerism, what people do.)

(3) What are the differences between present and past attitudes to life in the class she is describing?

(4) Rita thinks that 'there's somethin' wrong' about the life she describes. What is it?

(5) Why does Frank mention politics, do you think? Work out what is political about Rita's view here, in the context of class and education.

(6) What does Rita say she gains from coming to Frank, and why does her husband try to stop her?

Remember that you're looking for evidence about contexts here, not about the relationships between the characters. Consider particularly 'They hate it when one of them tries to break away'. What does this say about class and education?

Contexts of class and politics

This section includes two extracts from *Top Girls* by Caryl Churchill. Like *Educating Rita*, this play is also about class, and movement between classes, but more directly relates class to politics. Here's the first extract:

MARLENE: She's a tough lady, Maggie. I'd give her a job. / She just needs to hang in there. This country

JOYCE: You voted for them, did you?

MARLENE: needs to stop whining. / Monetarism is not stupid.

JOYCE: Drink your tea and shut up, pet.

MARLENE: It takes time, determination. No more slop. / And

JOYCE: Well I think they're filthy bastards.

MARLENE: who's got to drive it on? First woman prime minister. Terrifico. Aces. Right on. / You must admit. Certainly gets my vote.

JOYCE: What good's first woman if it's her? I suppose you'd have liked Hitler if he was a woman. Ms Hitler. Got a lot done, Hitlerina. / Great adventures.

MARLENE: Bosses still walking on the workers' faces? Still Dadda's little parrot? Haven't you learned to think for yourself? I believe in the individual. Look at me.

JOYCE: I am looking at you.

MARLENE: Come on, Joyce, we're not going to quarrel over politics.

JOYCE: We are though.

MARLENE: Forget I mentioned it. Not a word about the slimy unions will cross my lips.

[*Pause.*]

JOYCE: You say Mother had a wasted life.

MARLENE: Yes I do. Married to that bastard.

JOYCE: What sort of life did he have? / Working in the fields like

MARLENE: Violent life?

JOYCE: an animal. / Why wouldn't he want a drink?

MARLENE: Come off it.

JOYCE: You want a drink. He couldn't afford whisky.

MARLENE: I don't want to talk about him.

JOYCE: You started, I was talking about her. She had a rotten life because she had nothing. She went hungry.

MARLENE: She was hungry because he drank the money. / He used to hit her.

JOYCE: It's not all down to him. / Their lives were rubbish. They

MARLENE: She didn't hit him.

JOYCE: were treated like rubbish. He's dead and she'll die soon and what sort of life / did they have?

Marlene's comment about 'Bosses still walking on the workers' faces' raises issues of class and politics. She herself is a 'boss', though she doesn't always see herself this way. She thinks that Joyce's attitudes are her father's ('Still Dadda's little parrot?'), and that she can't escape from them. She contrasts her belief in 'the individual' with 'the slimy unions' – the word 'slimy' shows her attitude, and the word 'unions' contrasts directly in meaning with 'the individual'. The language so far is the language of class politics – 'bosses', 'workers', 'unions', 'the individual'.

The mention of Margaret Thatcher heightens the tension between Marlene and Joyce – 'I'd give her a job' and 'Certainly gets my vote' contrasting with 'You voted for them' and 'I think they're filthy bastards'. There are other political issues here, too, including economic politics, introduced with the reference to monetarism, and gender politics, with the comment about 'the first woman prime minister' and Joyce's response to it.

Marlene sees her parents' lives in terms of individuals – she hated her father, and characterises him as a violent drunk who 'wasted' her mother's life. Joyce's defence of her father, however, clearly relates to class. He worked in the fields 'like an animal' (suggesting economic exploitation), and drank as a result, which Joyce uses to attack Marlene's wealth: 'he couldn't afford whisky'. Her mother's life was 'rotten' because she was poor and hungry, and she sees them as a unit, representative of their class: 'What sort of life did they have?'

Here is the next extract from the play, which follows the first extract almost immediately in the text:

MARLENE: America, America, you're jealous. / I had to get out,

JOYCE: Jealous?

MARLENE: I knew when I was thirteen, out of their house, out of them, never let that happen to me, / never let him, make my own way, out.

JOYCE: Jealous of what you've done, you're ashamed of me if I came to your office, your smart friends, wouldn't you, I'm ashamed of you, think of nothing but yourself, you've got on, nothing's changed for most people / has it?

MARLENE: I hate the working class / which is what you're going

JOYCE: Yes you do.

MARLENE: to go on about now, it doesn't exist any more, it means lazy and stupid. / I don't like the way they talk. I don't

JOYCE: Come on, now we're getting it.

MARLENE: like beer guts and football vomit and saucy tits / and brothers and sisters –

JOYCE: I spit when I see a Rolls Royce, scratch it with my ring / Mercedes it was.

MARLENE: Oh very mature –

JOYCE: I hate the cows I work for / and their dirty dishes with blanquette of fucking veau.

MARLENE: and I will not be pulled down to their level by a flying picket and I won't be sent to Siberia / or a loony bin

JOYCE: No, you'll be on a yacht, you'll be head of Coca-Cola and you wait, the eighties is going to be stupendous all right because we'll get you lot off our backs –

MARLENE: just because I'm original. And I support Reagan even if he is a lousy movie star because the reds are swarming up his map and I want to be free in a free world –

JOYCE: What? / What?

MARLENE: I know what I mean / by that – not shut up here.

JOYCE: So don't be round here when it happens because if someone's kicking you I'll just laugh.

[*Silence.*]

MARLENE: I don't mean anything personal. I don't believe in class. Anyone can do anything if they've got what it takes.

ACTIVITY 22

Apply the model used in the previous extract and search for context here. Here are some ideas and questions to help you.

(1) What is Marlene's attitude to the working class here? How does she characterise how 'they' act and think? Look at the language she uses to describe 'them'.

(2) What is Joyce's attitude to 'smart' people and 'you lot' here? Look for the possessions and activities she selects, and the language she uses about them.

(3) How does Joyce interpret Marlene's belief in 'the individual'? When she says 'nothing's changed for most people', who is she thinking of? (There are several possibilities to explore here).

(4) Look carefully at the words Marlene uses for evidence that her views stem from her experiences at home. Look for terms that belong to the language of class politics, and for references to politics and economics and how they relate to the central context. Explore what Marlene means by each of the statements in her last speech in the extract.

After you've studied these two extracts from *Top Girls*, you should consider how the issues they raise appear in the rest of the play. This will give you the material to use in an exam response about the play.

Historical context

Many plays have historical contexts. For instance, *Top Girls* has a series of historical contexts that inform our attitudes to the characters in Act One, and another historical context in the attitudes to Thatcherism shown in the first of the two extracts presented above. *A Streetcar Named Desire* has a historical context too, in the changing social and economic order of postwar America.

The next extract provides a clearer example. It's from Robert Bolt's play *A Man for All Seasons*, set in the reign of Henry VIII at a time when the king and Sir Thomas More disagree about Henry's right to marry Anne Boleyn. At the opening of the play, the Chancellor of England is Cardinal Wolsey. More replaced Wolsey as Chancellor in 1529 but was executed in 1535.

WOLSEY: Where has he been? D'you know?

MORE: I, Your Grace?

WOLSEY: Oh, spare me your discretion. He's been to play in the muck again.

MORE: [*coldly*]: Indeed.

WOLSEY: Indeed! Indeed! Are you going to oppose me? [*Trumpet again.* WOLSEY *visibly relaxes.*] He's gone in. . . . [*Leaves window.*] All right, we'll plod. The King wants a son; what are you going to do about it?

MORE: [*dry murmur*]: I'm very sure the King needs no advice from me on what to do about it.

WOLSEY: [*from behind grips his shoulder fiercely*]: Thomas, we're alone. I give you my word. There's no one here.

MORE: I didn't suppose there was, Your Grace.

WOLSEY: Oh. [*Goes to table, sits, signs* MORE *to sit.* MORE *unsuspectingly obeys. Then, deliberately loud.*] Do you favour a change of dynasty, Sir Thomas? D'you think two Tudors is sufficient?

MORE: [*Starting up in horrified alarm*]: – For God's sake, Your Grace – !

WOLSEY: Then the King needs a son; I repeat what are you going to do about it?

MORE: [*steadily*]: I pray for it daily.

WOLSEY: [*snatches up candle and holds to* MORE's *face. Softly*]: God's death, he means it. . . . That thing out there's at least fertile, Thomas.

MORE: But she's not his wife.

WOLSEY: No, Catherine's his wife and she's as barren as brick. Are you going to pray for a miracle?

MORE: There *are* precedents.

WOLSEY: Yes. All right. Good. Pray. Pray by all means. But in addition to Prayer there is Effort. My effort's to secure a divorce. Have I your support or have I not?

MORE: [*sits*]: A dispensation was given so that the King might marry Queen Catherine, for state reasons. Now we are to ask the Pope to – dispense with his dispensation, also for state reasons?

You could identify several historical contexts here. Although Henry famously had many wives, he was not necessarily faithful to them. This is revealed here in Wolsey's remark 'He's been to play in the muck again'. This in turn affects our reading of Henry's behaviour in the play, such as his attitude to Margaret.

The desire for a son to secure the line, and therefore the succession, was a driving force for Henry; it appears in 'The King wants a son', and specifically in 'D'you think two Tudors is sufficient?' This historical necessity drives the action of the play, in that it drives Henry's actions and the political necessity to take More with him. The problem of Catherine's barrenness caused Henry to go against the Pope's wishes and to found the Church of England, referred to elsewhere in the play. Henry's actions caused a huge rift in the Church in England and cost many lives, including that of Sir Thomas More. This informs much of the political manoeuvring in the play, and explains the importance of the Spanish characters, who support both the Pope and Catherine's nephew, the King of Spain.

There's also a religious context here, seen in the contrast between Wolsey's and More's attitudes to prayer.

Now apply the same criteria to another extract from the play:

MORE: Must you wear those clothes, Will?

ROPER: Yes, I must.

MORE: Why?

ROPER: The time has come for decent men to declare their allegiance!

MORE: And what allegiance are those designed to express?

ROPER: My allegiance to the Church.

MORE: Well, you *look* like a Spaniard.

ROPER: All credit to Spain then!

MORE: You wouldn't last six months in Spain. You'd have been burned alive in Spain, during your heretic period.

ROPER: I suppose you have the right to remind me of it. [*Points accusingly.*] That chain of office that *you* wear is a degradation.

MORE: [*glances down at it*]: I've told you. If the bishops in Convocation submitted this morning, I'll take it off. . . . It's no degradation. Great men have worn this.

ROPER: When d'you expect to hear from Canterbury?

MORE: About now. The Archbishop promised me an immediate message.

ROPER: [*recommences pacing*]: I don't see what difference Convocation can make. The Church is already a wing of the Palace is it not? The King is already its 'Supreme Head'! Is he not?

MORE: No.

ROPER: [*is startled*]: You are denying the Act of Supremacy!

MORE: No, I'm not; the Act states that the King –

ROPER: – is Supreme Head of the Church in England.

MORE: Supreme Head of the Church in England – [*Underlining the words.*] 'so far as the law of God allows'. How far the law of God does allow it remains a matter of opinion, since the Act doesn't state it.

ACTIVITY 23

You may need to do some research to gain a full understanding of the issues raised here – you can see from the text that they're significant. The following points should help:

- What is the significance of the references to Spain?

- 'You'd have been burned alive . . . during your heretic period' refers to Roper's attitudes earlier in the play – but what are the historical references here? Of course, this adds to the violence that is always the background to the play.

- What have the 'bishops in Convocation' submitted to? What difference does this make to More's position?

- Roper says that 'The Church is already a wing of the Palace'. What does he mean? What is the power relationship that he describes here? Examine its importance both historically and in the play.

- Look up the Act of Supremacy.

- There's another type of social context raised in the last sentence of the extract, which is the law. How is this important in the rest of the play?

Cultural contexts

Most plays have a cultural context as well as a social context, in that they're set within a particular culture. When the cultural context affects our reading of the play's meanings it becomes something we need to explore. Here's an example from *A Streetcar Named Desire*, by Tennessee Williams:

STANLEY: Delicate piece she is.

STELLA: She is. She was. You didn't know Blanche as a girl. Nobody, nobody, was tender and trusting as she was. But people like you abused her, and forced her to change.

[*He crosses into the bedroom, ripping off his shirt, and changes into a brilliant silk bowling shirt. She follows him.*]

Do you think you're going bowling now?

STANLEY: Sure.

STELLA: You're not going bowling. [*She catches hold of his shirt.*] Why did you do this to her?

STANLEY: I done nothing to no one. Let go of my shirt. You've torn it.

STELLA: I want to know why first. Tell me why.

STANLEY: When we first met, me and you, you thought I was common. How right you was, baby. I was common as dirt. You showed me the snapshot of the place with the columns. I pulled you down off them columns and how you loved

> it, having them coloured lights going! And wasn't we happy together, wasn't it all okay till she showed here?
>
> [STELLA *makes a slight movement. Her look goes suddenly inward as if some interior voice had called her name. She begins a slow, shuffling progress from the bedroom to the kitchen, leaning and resting on the back of the chair and then on the edge of a table with a blind look and listening expression.* STANLEY, *finishing with his shirt, is unaware of her reaction.*]
>
> And wasn't we happy together? Wasn't it all okay? Till she showed here. Hoity-toity, describing me as an ape. [*He suddenly notices the change in* STELLA.] Hey, what is it, Stell? [*He crosses to her.*]
>
> STELLA: [*quietly*]: Take me to the hospital.

The dramatic tensions between Stanley, Stella and Blanche in this play are fed by cultural differences, which is why the cultural contexts feed our understanding of the play.

For example, 'tender and trusting' is a description of Blanche's character as a girl – but this is not just the opposite of Stanley as an individual, who despises both ideas. 'Tender and trusting' belongs to the culture of Belle Reve, the Dubois' country estate, and the old Southern gentry, whereas the new world Stanley lives in is hard and driving, where every man looks out for himself. Of course, there's a historical context here too.

The 'brilliant silk bowling shirt' is cultural in two ways. The gaudy colours of the shirt – Stanley is described as a 'gaudy seed-bearer' on his first entrance – contrast with Blanche's delicate colours. Bowling belongs to the new world, not the old. Stanley is as proud of his shirt – 'Let go of my shirt. You've torn it' – as Blanche is of her dresses.

Stanley's culture was seen as 'common' by Stella, and is now by Blanche. Stanley sees 'the place with the columns' as representing Stella (and Blanche), and a place that thinks of itself as better than him. He pulled her down off the columns, and sees Blanche's attitude to him as 'hoity-toity'.

The 'coloured lights going' belongs to Stanley's culture – he contrasts it directly with Belle Reve – and represents sexual activity between him and Stella, which she enjoyed. Stella's problem, of course, is that she has changed cultures, and is now caught between them. She accepts the casual domestic violence of the neighbourhood, for instance, which Blanche cannot understand. The mention of the coloured lights is immediately followed by the signs of Stella going into labour – the outcome of the change of culture. Stanley has been too busy with his shirt to notice!

Now read this second extract from the same play:

BLANCHE: May I – speak – *plainly?*
STELLA: Yes, do. Go ahead. As plainly as you want to.

            [*Outside a train approaches. They are silent till the noise subsides. They are both in the bedroom.*
            Under cover of the train's noise STANLEY *enters from outside. He stands unseen by the women, holding some packages in his arms, and overhears their following conversation. He wears an undershirt and grease-stained seersucker pants.*]

BLANCHE: Well – if you'll forgive me – he's *common!*
STELLA: Why, yes, I suppose he is.
BLANCHE: Suppose! You can't have forgotten that much of our bringing up, Stella, that you just *suppose* that any part of a gentleman's in his nature! *Not one particle, no!* Oh, if he was just – *ordinary!* Just *plain* – but good and wholesome, but – *no.* There's something downright – *bestial* – about him! You're hating me saying this, aren't you?
STELLA: [*coldly*]: Go on and say it all, Blanche.
BLANCHE: He acts like an animal, has an animal's habits! Eats like one, moves like one, talks like one! There's even something – sub-human – something not quite to the stage of humanity yet! Yes, something – ape-like about him, like one of those pictures I've seen in – anthropological studies! Thousands and thousands of years have passed him right by, and there he is – Stanley Kowalski – survivor of the Stone Age! Bearing the raw meat home from the kill in the jungle! And you – *you* here – *waiting* for him! Maybe he'll strike you or maybe grunt and kiss you! That is, if kisses have been discovered yet! Night falls and the other apes gather! There in the front of the cave, all grunting like him, and swilling and gnawing and hulking! His poker night! – you call it – this party of apes! Somebody growls – some creature snatches at something – the fight is on! *God*! Maybe we are a long way from being made in God's image, but Stella – my sister – there has been some progress since then! Such things as art – as poetry and music – such kinds of new light have come into the world since then! In some kinds of people some tenderer feelings have had some little beginning! That we have got to make *grow!* And *cling* to, and hold as our flag! In this dark march toward whatever it is we're approaching. . . *Don't – don't hang back with the brutes!*

            [*Another train passes outside.* STANLEY *hesitates, licking his lips. Then suddenly he turns stealthily about and withdraws through the front door. The women are still unaware of his presence. When the train has passed he calls through the closed front door.*]

STANLEY: Hey! Hey, Stella!
STELLA: [*who has listened gravely to* BLANCHE]: Stanley!

BLANCHE: Stell, I —

[*But* STELLA *has gone to the front door.* STANLEY *enters casually with his packages.*]

STANLEY: Hiyuh, Stella, Blanche back?

STELLA: Yes, she's back.

STANLEY: Hiyuh, Blanche. [*He grins at her.*]

STELLA: You must've got under the car.

STANLEY: Them darn mechanics at Fritz's don't know their can from third base!

[STELLA *has embraced him with both arms, fiercely, and full in the view of* BLANCHE. *He laughs and clasps her head to him. Over her head he grins through the curtains at* BLANCHE.

As the lights fade away, with a lingering brightness on their embrace, the music of the 'blue piano' and trumpet and drums is heard.]

ACTIVITY 24

Explore the cultural context in this extract. Here are some guidelines.

Look at the stage directions. What, for example, is the significance of Stanley's dress (remember you're thinking about cultural context here)? How would you interpret the description of his movements? How does the music belong to this culture?

How does Blanche characterise the culture of the sisters' 'bringing up'? Look at the words she uses to describe it, the interests belonging to it, and the feelings it engendered. Blanche sees Stanley as 'an ape', 'sub-human'. How does she describe his culture? Look carefully at the abusive words she uses, the mentions of particular interests belonging to his culture, and the feelings (or lack of them) engendered by it. Where does Stella stand in this battle of opposites? Look for clues in the extract.

Social/moral contexts

Many plays are concerned, naturally, with the morality of the period in which they are set – the rules, or codes of conduct, that affect behaviour. For instance, this type of context appears in *A Man for All Seasons* in the debate about private against public behaviour illustrated by the next extract:

MORE: – I've already expressed my opinion on this –

WOLSEY: – Then, good night! Oh, your conscience is your own affair; but you're a statesman! Do you *remember* the Yorkist Wars?

MORE: Very clearly.

WOLSEY: Let him die without an heir and we'll have them back again. Let him die without an heir and this 'peace' you think so much of will go out like that! [*Extinguishes candle.*] Very well, then England needs an heir; certain measures, perhaps regrettable, perhaps not – [*pompous*] there is much in the Church that *needs* reformation, Thomas – [MORE *smiles.*] All right, regrettable! But necessary, to get us an heir! Now explain how you as Councillor of England can obstruct those measures for the sake of your own, private, conscience.

MORE: Well . . . I believe, when statesmen forsake their own private conscience for the sake of their public duties . . . they lead their country by a short route to chaos. [*During this speech he relights the candle with another.*] And we shall have my prayers to fall back on.

WOLSEY: You'd like that, wouldn't you? To govern the country by prayers?

MORE: Yes, I should.

WOLSEY: I'd like to be there when you try.

In this extract, More's conscience is the problem – for him, his family, the King, and his friends, as it is throughout the play. It will not allow him to behave differently in public from the way he thinks and feels in private. This is dramatised by exploring the issue through his own words: 'I believe, when statesmen forsake their own private conscience for the sake of their public duties . . .' It is also dramatised by showing its opposite in action. It's clear that characters such as Wolsey, Cromwell and Rich have no such problems. When Wolsey says that 'your conscience is your own affair; but you're a statesman!' he implies that the two things are different – that a statesman cannot always act according to his conscience. His reasons are those of expediency; to ignore conscience will avoid a repetition of civil war.

Bolt's language highlights the concept. For example, the word 'private' in 'your own, private, conscience' shows that this is merely a private matter that need not impinge on public policy, in More's view. More's position is given its clearest statement in the play here. His deep religious belief informs his position – governing the country by prayers is an expression of the private governing the public, rather than the other way round. More's 'Yes, I should' is clearly serious – a position that the realist cardinal cannot accept: 'I'd like to be there when you try'.

Now look at this next extract from the play in the same way:

ALICE: What's this? You crossed him.

MORE: Somewhat.

ALICE: Why?

MORE: [*apologetic*]: I couldn't find the other way.

ALICE: [*angrily*]: You're too nice altogether, Thomas!

MORE: Woman, mind your house.

ALICE: I *am* minding my house!

MORE: [*takes in her anxiety*]: Well, Alice. What would you *want* me to do?

ALICE: Be ruled! If you won't rule him, be ruled!

MORE: [*quietly*]: I neither could nor would rule my King. [*Pleasantly.*] But there's a little . . . little, area . . . where I must rule myself. It's very little – less to him than a tennis court. [*Her face is still full of foreboding: he sighs.*] Look; it was eight o'clock. At eight o'clock, Lady Anne likes to dance.

ALICE: [*relieved*]: Oh?

MORE: I think so.

ALICE: [*irritation*]: And *you* stand between them!

MORE: I? What stands between them is a sacrament of the Church. I'm less important than you think, Alice.

ALICE: [*appealing*]: Thomas, stay friends with him.

MORE: Whatever can be done by smiling, you may rely on me to do.

ALICE: You don't know *how* to flatter.

MORE: I flatter very well! My recipe's beginning to be widely copied. It's the basic syrup with just a soupçon of discreet impudence. . . .

ALICE: [*still uneasy*]: I wish he'd eaten here. . . .

MORE: Yes – we shall be living on that 'simple supper' of yours for a fortnight. [*She won't laugh.*] Alice. . . . [*She won't turn.*] Alice. . . . [*She turns.*] Set your mind at rest – this [*tapping himself*] is not the stuff of which martyrs are made.

ACTIVITY 25

Use the following questions to help you understand how this moral issue is developed in the play. Remember to think about what characters say, the language they use, and what they do.

- Why can't Sir Thomas 'find the other way'? What would 'the other way' entail for him?

- What does Alice mean by 'I *am* minding my house'? Think about the results of More's refusal to go against his private beliefs – this is how an understanding of the context informs a reading of the play.

- More says 'there's a little . . . area . . . where I must rule myself'. What is this area? What does More imply when he says that for the king 'it's less to him than a tennis court'?

- What stands between the king and Lady Anne, according to More? What has it to do with his private belief? What does he mean by 'I'm less important than you think'?

- How far is More prepared to go? Think about his attitude to speaking and not speaking in the rest of the play – it stems from this.

- Referring to himself, More says 'this is not the stuff of which martyrs are made'. Why does Sir Thomas become a martyr?

To answer the last two questions you'll need to know the rest of the play – but you can see how, in tackling your set play, the context can be explored in the rest of it.

Philosophical contexts

Plays often have a philosophical framework or context that we need to recognise and explore for a full understanding of the piece. Look at this extract from Samuel Beckett's *Waiting for Godot*:

VLADIMIR: I don't know what to think any more.
ESTRAGON: My feet! [*He sits down, tries to take off his boots.*] Help me!
VLADIMIR: Was I sleeping, while the others suffered? Am I sleeping now? Tomorrow, when I wake, or think I do, what shall I say of today? That with Estragon my friend, at this place, until the fall of night, I waited for Godot? That Pozzo passed, with his carrier, and that he spoke to us? Probably. But in all that what truth will there be? [*Estragon, having struggled with his boots in vain, is dozing off again. Vladimir stares at him.*] He'll know nothing. He'll tell me about the blows he received and I'll give him a carrot. [*Pause.*] Astride of a grave and a difficult birth. Down in the hole, lingeringly, the grave-digger puts on the forceps. We have time to grow old. The air is full of our cries. [*He listens.*] But habit is a great deadener. [*He looks again at Estragon.*] At me too someone is looking, of me too someone is saying, he is sleeping, he knows nothing, let him sleep on. [*Pause.*] I can't go on! [*Pause.*] What have I said?

[*He goes feverishly to and fro, halts finally at extreme left, broods.*]

In this extract, Vladimir struggles to make sense of life. 'I don't know what to think any more' indicates his confusion, about life, and introduces his struggle to form a philosophy. Estragon's simple cry of 'Help me!' reminds the audience theatrically of one of the philosophical tenets most often referred to in the play, the need to help each other in adversity.

Vladimir is particularly concerned about consciousness ('Was I sleeping?'), conscience ('while the others suffered'), the nature of existence ('what shall I say of today?'), and truth ('what truth will there be?'). These are clearly philosophical concerns, each of which is looked at elsewhere in the play, in words and actions. He recognises the repetitiveness of life ('He'll tell me about the blows he received and I'll give him a carrot'), which is exemplified in the play in words, actions and structure, in the way that the second half of the play so closely echoes the first. He also broods on Pozzo's remark, made immediately before the passage in the extract, 'They give birth astride the grave'. The birth is 'difficult'; it is the grave-digger who 'puts on the forceps', implying a painful delivery, and we have time only to 'grow old'. Life here is for suffering – 'The air is full of our cries'.

Finally, as he looks at Estragon, he imagines someone watching him – another repetition. He implies his own (and mankind's) ignorance, and perhaps another, perhaps higher, presence. God? Godot? The stage presence of the sleeping figure of Estragon is important here – the audience can see a representation of his thought. The actions – 'feverish', brooding – imply the force and difficulty of thought: a philosophical view about the difficulties of philosophy.

Here's another extract from the play to think about. This is an extraordinary speech, which has a language context too (see below). You might think that there are no thoughts expressed clearly here (which is probably true), and that therefore it is difficult to say anything about the philosophical context. However, what we can see here is that philosophy permeates the text, even in outbursts such as this.

LUCKY: Given the existence as uttered forth in the public works of Puncher and Wattmann of a personal God quaquaquaqua with white beard quaquaquaqua outside time without extension who from the heights of divine apathia divine athambia divine aphasia loves us dearly with some exceptions for reasons unknown but time will tell and suffers like the divine Miranda with those who for reasons unknown but time will tell are plunged in torment plunged in fire whose fire flames if that continues and who can doubt it will fire the firmament that is to say blast hell to heaven so blue still and calm so calm with a calm which even though intermittent is better than nothing but not so fast and considering what is more that as a result of the labours left unfinished crowned by the Acacacacademy of Anthropopopometry of Essy-in-Possy of Testew and Cunard it is established beyond all doubt all other doubt than that which clings to the labours of men that as a result of the labours unfinished of Testew and Cunard it is established as hereinafter but not so fast for reasons unknown that as a result of the public works of Puncher and Wattmann it is established beyond all doubt that in view of the labours of Fartov and Belcher left unfinished for reasons unknown of Testew and Cunard left unfinished it is established what many deny that man in Possy of Testew and Cunard that man in Essy that man in short that man in brief in spite of the strides of alimentation and defecation is seen to waste and pine waste and pine and concurrently simultaneously what is more for reasons unknown in spite of the strides of physical culture the practice of sports such as tennis football running cycling swimming flying floating riding gliding conating camogie skating tennis of all kinds dying flying sports of all sorts autumn summer winter winter tennis of all kinds hockey of all sorts penicilline and succedanea in a word I resume and concurrently simultaneously for reasons unknown to shrink and dwindle in spite of the tennis I resume flying gliding golf over nine and eighteen holes tennis of all sorts in a word for reasons unknown in Feckham Peckham Fulham Clapham namely concurrently simultaneously what is more for reasons unknown but time will tell to shrink and dwindle I resume Fulham Clapham in a word the dead loss per caput since the death of Bishop Berkeley being to the tune of one inch four ounce per caput approximately by and large more or less to the nearest decimal good measure round figures stark naked in the stockinged feet in Connemara in a word for reasons unknown no matter what matter the facts are there and considering what is more much more grave that in the light of the labours lost of Steinweg and Peterman it appears what is more much more grave that in the light the light the light of the labours lost of Steinweg and Peterman that in the plains in the mountains by the seas by the rivers running water running fire the air is the same and then the earth namely the air and then the earth in the great cold the great dark the air and the earth abode of stones in the great cold alas alas in the year of their Lord six hundred and something the air the earth the sea the earth abode of stones in the great deeps the great cold on sea on land and in the air I resume for reasons unknown in spite of the tennis the facts are there but time will tell I resume alas alas on on in short in fine on on abode of stones who can doubt it I resume but not so fast I resume the skull to shrink and waste and concurrently simultaneously what is more for reasons unknown in spite of the tennis on on the beard the flames the tears the stones so blue so calm alas alas on on the skull the skull the skull the skull in Connemara in spite of the tennis the labours abandoned left unfinished graver still abode of stones in a word I resume alas alas abandoned unfinished the skull the skull in Connemara in spite of the tennis the skull alas the stones Cunard [*mêlée, final vociferations*] tennis . . . the stones . . . so calm . . . Cunard . . . unfinished . . .

POZZO: His hat!

[VLADIMIR *seizes* LUCKY'S *hat. Silence of* LUCKY. *He falls. Silence*]

ACTIVITY 26

Search the speech for words and phrases that suggest a philosophical context, particularly those you see echoed in the rest of the text. For instance, 'time will tell' (repeated) is echoed in Vladimir's and Estragon's preoccupation with the time of day, and what time may reveal – and this is repeated in the two halves. What other suggestions of a philosophical context can you find?

Feminism

Sometimes plays are written within the context of a particular attitude or philosophy, such as feminism. Once again, recognising and exploring this context will enrich your understanding of the text. Here's another extract from Caryl Churchill's *Top Girls*.

ISABELLA: Australia to the Sandwich Isles, I fell in love with the sea. There were rats in the cabin and ants in the food but suddenly it was like a new world. I woke up every morning happy, knowing there would be nothing to annoy me. No nervousness. No dressing.

NIJO: Don't you like getting dressed? I adored my clothes. / When I was chosen to give sake to His Majesty's brother,

MARLENE: You had prettier colours than Isabella.

NIJO: the Emperor Kameyana, on his formal visit, I wore raw silk pleated trousers and a seven-layered gown in shades of red, and two outer garments, / yellow lined with green and a light

MARLENE: Yes, all that silk must have been very . . .

[*The* WAITRESS *starts to clear the first course.*]

JOAN: I dressed as a boy when I left home.

NIJO: green jacket. Lady Betto had a five-layered gown in shades of green and purple.

ISABELLA: You dressed as a boy?

MARLENE: Of course, / for safety.

JOAN: It was easy, I was only twelve. Also women weren't / allowed in the library. We wanted to study in Athens.

MARLENE: You ran away alone?

JOAN: No, not alone, I went with my friend. / He was sixteen

NIJO: Ah, an elopement.

JOAN: but I thought I knew more science than he did and almost as much philosophy.

ISABELLA: Well I always travelled as a lady and I repudiated strongly any suggestion in the press that I was other than feminine.

MARLENE: I don't wear trousers in the office. / I could but I don't.

ISABELLA: There was no great danger to a woman of my age and appearance.

MARLENE: And you got away with it, Joan?

JOAN: I did then.

[*The* WAITRESS *starts to bring the main course.*]

MARLENE: And nobody noticed anything?

JOAN: They noticed I was a very clever boy. / And when I

MARLENE: I couldn't have kept pretending for so long.

JOAN: shared a bed with my friend, that was ordinary – two poor students in a lodging house. I think I forgot I was pretending.

ISABELLA: Rocky Mountain Jim, Mr Nugent, showed me no disrespect. He found it interesting, I think, that I could make scones and also lasso cattle. Indeed he declared his love for me, which was most distressing.

In this passage Isabella clearly exults in escaping society's constraints on her as a woman. She falls in love not with a man, but with the sea. It was 'like a new world': the freedom is more important to her than the rats and ants, privations which a woman might traditionally be expected to hate. What has annoyed her has been 'nervousness' and 'dressing' – the weight of social expectations of her, in behaviour and dress. Nijo, on the other hand, appears to be an 'unreconstructed' woman here, not in her enjoyment of clothes, but in the fact that she dresses for men, apparently, rather than herself. It is later in the Act that she emerges as a feminist figure.

Dress brings in Pope Joan, who had to dress as male in order to be accepted, not just as Pope, but as someone who would be allowed in a library. This exemplifies male attitudes to female study, further undermined by Joan's view that 'I thought I knew more science than he did'. She was noticed as clever – but as 'a very clever boy' – presumably she couldn't have been recognised as 'a very clever girl'.

Isabella hints at media slurs on women who act independently: 'I repudiated strongly any suggestion in the press that I was other than feminine'. Marlene articulates a modern view, of having the right to choose: 'I don't wear trousers in the office. / I could do but I don't.' Mr Nugent found it 'interesting' that Isabella could 'make scones and also lasso cattle'. Isabella again breaks the traditional female mould, and is admired for it. She is 'distressed' when Mr Nugent declares his love!

Here's another extract from the play to look at:

> NIJO: They wouldn't let me into the palace when he was dying. I hid in the room with his coffin, then I couldn't find where I'd left my shoes, I ran after the funeral procession in bare feet, I couldn't keep up. When I got there it was over, a few wisps of smoke in the sky, that's all that was left of him. What I want to know is, if I'd still been at court, would I have been allowed to wear full mourning?
>
> MARLENE: I'm sure you would.
>
> NIJO: Why do you say that? You don't know anything about it. Would I have been allowed to wear full mourning?
>
> ISABELLA: How can people live in this dim pale island and wear our hideous clothes? I cannot and will not live the life of a lady.
>
> NIJO: I'll tell you something that made me angry. I was eighteen, at the Full Moon Ceremony. They make a special rice gruel and stir it with their sticks, and then they beat their women across the loins so they'll have sons and not daughters. So the Emperor beat us all / very hard as usual – that's not it,
>
> MARLENE: What a sod.
>
> NIJO: Marlene, that's normal, what made us angry, he told his attendants they could beat us too. Well they had a wonderful time. / So Lady Genki and I made a plan, and the ladies all hid
>
> [*The* WAITRESS *has entered with coffees.*]
>
> MARLENE: I'd like another brandy please. Better make it six.

NIJO: in his rooms, and Lady Mashimizu stood guard with a stick at the door, and when His Majesty came in Genki seized him and I beat him till he cried out and promised he would never order anyone to hit us again. Afterwards there was a terrible fuss. The nobles were horrified. 'We wouldn't even dream of stepping on your Majesty's shadow.' And I had hit him with a stick. Yes, I hit him with a stick.

ACTIVITY 27

Look through the extract for anything that shows feminist attitudes and ideas. The following questions should help you to see how the feminist context is embedded in the text.

(1) What was Nijo not allowed to do, and what action does she take? (2) What does make Nijo angry and what doesn't – and in each case, why? (3) What is the purpose of the beatings? What does it imply about the society's values? (4) What is Nijo proud of? How does Churchill show her pride, and what does it say about Nijo? (5) What does Isabella mean by 'I cannot and will not live the life of a lady'? (Remember that her attitude is nothing to do with being feminine or not – she resents being thought of as unfeminine.) What does she mean by 'the life of a lady', do you think? (Notice that she uses the word 'lady', not woman.)

Dramatic/theatrical context

Plays are written to be performed. During performance, things happen to the audience that they can't experience in the same way by simply reading the text. In this sense, every performance of a play creates a dramatic/theatrical context, in which the audience can see dramatic and theatrical elements at work. This means that a performance of any play should be looked at in its dramatic context; you'll find suggestions about how to approach this in Module 3 on Shakespeare.

That approach, however, is really only suitable for coursework – not every candidate can be expected to attend performances of every play they might study in order to be examined on it. Some plays, however, have such clear dramatic elements that they can be looked at in class and in exams. As an example, here's another extract from *A Streetcar Named Desire*.

STANLEY: Catch!
STELLA: What?
STANLEY: Meat!

[*He heaves the package at her. She cries out in protest but manages to catch it: then she laughs breathlessly. Her husband and his companion have already started back around the corner.*]

STELLA: [*calling after him*]: Stanley! Where are you going?
STANLEY: Bowling!

STELLA: Can I come watch?

STANLEY: Come on. [*He goes out.*]

STELLA: Be over soon. [*To the white woman.*]: Hello, Eunice. How are you?

EUNICE: I'm all right. Tell Steve to get him a poor boy's sandwich 'cause nothing's left here.

    [*They all laugh; the* NEGRO WOMAN *does not stop.* STELLA *goes out.*]

NEGRO WOMAN: What was that package he th'ew at 'er? [*She rises from steps, laughing louder.*]

EUNICE: You hush, now!

NEGRO WOMAN: Catch *what*!

    [*She continues to laugh.* BLANCHE *comes around the corner, carrying a valise. She looks at a slip of paper, then at the building, then again at the slip and again at the building. Her expression is one of shocked disbelief. Her appearance is incongruous to this setting. She is daintily dressed in a white suit with a fluffy bodice, necklace and earrings of pearl, white gloves and hat, looking as if she were arriving at a summer tea or cocktail party in the garden district. She is about five years older than* STELLA. *Her delicate beauty must avoid a strong light. There is something about her uncertain manner, as well as her white clothes, that suggests a moth.*

The 'meat' that Stanley throws is described in an earlier stage direction as a 'red-stained package'. As such it symbolises Stanley's primitive role as hunter/gatherer, and he throws it to Stella. The primitive nature suggested is underlined by speech patterns: notice the single word – often single syllable – sentences here.

The package of meat has significance as a phallic symbol, too; soon Stella will be revealed as pregnant. In a recent production, the meat within must have been a large piece of rolled topside of beef, judging by the shape. The visual message about Stanley was clear, and informed the audience's whole perception of him. This is his first appearance, after all.

The message of the meat is underlined by dialogue – the negro woman recognises its significance, and her laughter helps to establish the mood and values of the neighbourhood. In other words, there are several dramatic elements working together here.

The appearance of Blanche is meaningful even before she speaks, as indicated in the stage directions: 'Her appearance is incongruous to this setting' signals the beginning of the conflict that shapes the play. The colours of white (repeated three times) and pearl contrast strongly with Stanley's bowling jacket. 'A summer tea or cocktail party in the garden district' does not suit this place, or time of day; and 'delicate', 'daintily', suggest someone quite at odds with Stanley's attitude and manner. The reference to a moth is an instruction to the actress, as well as an image that helps to define Blanche's behaviour and tragedy. Her movement contrasts with Stanley's confidence – he throws the meat and immediately starts back. The negro woman's coarse laugh continues as Blanche arrives – a simple dramatic device to create an effect, juxtaposing Blanche against the setting.

Now look for comparable signs of the dramatic/theatrical context in this next extract from the play:

BLANCHE: Then I found out. In the worst of all possible ways. By coming suddenly into a room that I thought was empty – which wasn't empty, but had two people in it . . .

[*A locomotive is heard approaching outside. She claps her hands to her ears and crouches over. The headlight of the locomotive glares into the room as it thunders past. As the noise recedes she straightens slowly and continues speaking.*]

Afterwards we pretended that nothing had been discovered. Yes, the three of us drove out to Moon Lake Casino, very drunk and laughing all the way.

[*Polka music sounds, in a minor key faint with distance.*]

We danced the Varsouviana! Suddenly in the middle of the dance the boy I had married broke away from me and ran out of the casino. A few moments later – a shot!

[*The Polka stops abruptly. BLANCHE rises stiffly. Then the Polka resumes in a major key.*]

I ran out – all did – all ran and gathered about the terrible thing at the edge of the lake! I couldn't get near for the crowding. Then somebody caught my arm. 'Don't go any closer! Come back! You don't want to see!' 'See? See what!' Then I heard voices say – Allan! Allan! The Grey boy! He'd stuck the revolver into his mouth, and fired – so that the back of his head had been – blown away!

[*She sways and covers her face.*]

It was because – on the dance-floor – unable to stop myself – I'd suddenly said – 'I know! I know! You disgust me . . .' And then the searchlight which had been turned on the world was turned off again and never for one moment since has there been any light that's stronger than this – kitchen – candle. . .

[*MITCH gets up awkwardly and moves towards her a little. The Polka music increases. MITCH stands beside her.*]

MITCH: [*drawing her slowly into his arms*]: You need somebody. And I need somebody, too. Could it be – you and me, Blanche?

[*She stares at him vacantly for a moment. Then with a soft cry huddles in his embrace. She makes a sobbing effort to speak but the words won't come. He kisses her forehead and her eyes and finally her lips. The Polka tune fades out. Her breath is drawn and released in long, grateful sobs.*]

BLANCHE: Sometimes – there's God – so quickly!

ACTIVITY 28

Use these notes and questions to help you decide how the dramatic/theatrical context informs the audience's interpretations of the play:

- The sound of the locomotive is 'real', unlike the other sounds in the extract, which are in Blanche's head and unheard by Mitch. Why has Williams introduced this element here? Think of the effect on Blanche, particularly of its light 'glaring' into the room and illuminating her. There are a number of possible interpretations. For example, think about what this extract reveals about Blanche and link to her associations with light throughout the play.

- When the polka music first appears, how does Williams make it clear that it is in Blanche's head? Why does the music change from minor to major key? Think about the difference in what the audience would hear.

- The searchlight of the locomotive is now used as an image that the audience will connect with because they've seen it already. What does Blanche mean by the 'searchlight' here? What does this explain about her behaviour, and her attitude to light?

- Why does the polka tune fade out when it does? What does Blanche mean by 'Sometimes – there's God'?

This passage contains the clearest explanation in the play of the polka tune and the shot, but they're used at several other points. To understand fully how Williams uses them, you need to find and explore the other moments.

You could look for this context in any of the plays mentioned so far in this module. For instance, look at the Common Man in *A Man for All Seasons*, Willy's 'voices' or music in *Death of a Salesman*, or Vladimir and Estragon's hats and boots routines, or their entries and re-entries, in *Waiting for Godot*.

Language context

The study of language in a play might seem to belong to Assessment Objective 3 – 'the ways in which writers' choices of form, structure and language shape meanings'. But in some plays language itself becomes an issue, so an understanding of the writer's use of language is necessary for a full understanding of the play's contexts. Beckett constantly plays with language forms in *Waiting for Godot*, so it's useful to recognise some of the techniques he uses. Here's an extract that is typical of much of the play's dialogue:

ESTRAGON: [*chewing*]: I asked you a question.
VLADIMIR: Ah.
ESTRAGON: Did you reply?
VLADIMIR: How's the carrot.
ESTRAGON: It's a carrot.

VLADIMIR:	So much the better, so much the better. [*Pause.*] What was it you wanted to know?
ESTRAGON:	I've forgotten. [*Chews.*] That's what annoys me. [*He looks at the carrot appreciatively, dangles it between finger and thumb.*] I'll never forget this carrot. [*He sucks the end of it meditatively.*] Ah yes, now I remember.
VLADIMIR:	Well?
ESTRAGON:	[*his mouth full, vacuously*]: We're not tied!
VLADIMIR:	I don't hear a word you're saying.
ESTRAGON:	[*chews, swallows*] I'm asking you if we're tied.
VLADIMIR:	Tied?
ESTRAGON:	Ti-ed.
VLADIMIR:	How do you mean tied?
ESTRAGON:	Down.
VLADIMIR:	But to whom. By whom?
ESTRAGON:	To your man.
VLADIMIR:	To Godot? Tied to Godot? What an idea! No question of it. [*Pause.*] For the moment.
ESTRAGON:	His name is Godot?
VLADIMIR:	I think so.
ESTRAGON:	Fancy that. [*He raises what remains of the carrot by the stub of leaf, twirls it before his eyes.*] Funny, the more you eat the worse it gets.
VLADIMIR:	With me it's just the opposite.
ESTRAGON:	In other words?
VLADIMIR:	I get used to the muck as I go along.
ESTRAGON:	[*after prolonged reflection*]: Is that the opposite?
VLADIMIR:	Question of temperament.
ESTRAGON:	Of character.
VLADIMIR:	Nothing you can do about it.
ESTRAGON:	No use struggling.
VLADIMIR:	One is what one is.
ESTRAGON:	No use wriggling.
VLADIMIR:	The essential doesn't change.
ESTRAGON:	Nothing to be done. [*He proffers the remains of the carrot to Vladimir.*] Like to finish it?

In reply to Estragon's question about a question, Vladimir asks him a question. Estragon's question was about their enslavement to Godot; Vladimir's is about a carrot. Vladimir's remark 'so much the better' is designed for weightier matters than carrots. When Vladimir asks for the question again, Estragon has forgotten it; only when he muses about never forgetting the carrot does he remember the question. Questions, question forms, and the opposites of forgetting and remembering are all juxtaposed with carrots, which gives the word play its absurd edge. When Estragon finally remembers, his words are unheard – because of the carrot.

Estragon has to divide the word 'Ti-ed' into syllables to be understood, and then to add a qualifier, 'down', to make sense of it for the listener. Vladimir's 'to whom? By whom?' plays with prepositions. When Vladimir finally responds to the question, his reply 'No question of it' continues to play with the word 'question' and the idea of questioning. Estragon turns an expected phrase on its head with 'the more you eat the worse it gets', though as only the carrot leaf seems to be left this is presumably true. He wants Vladimir's 'it's just the opposite' explained 'In other words', and when he gets the reply he questions the common phrase again – 'Is that the opposite?' – after deep thought.

This leads to a series of words and phrases suggesting abstract and philosophical concepts – temperament, character, the pointlessness of struggle, the impossibility of change – all emanating from the act of eating the carrot. And Estragon brings the sequence to an end by reminding the audience of its beginnings: 'Like to finish it?' Elsewhere the two tramps meditate in a more serious context about life via trivial concerns. Here Beckett uses an array of language techniques to point up the absurdity of the discussion, and to create humour.

There are other features of the language of *Waiting for Godot* that you could look at. Look back at Lucky's speech on pages 96–7. It's still daunting, in terms of language – you can't say much about its sentencing and paragraphing, except that there isn't any. This is a feature in itself, of course.

ACTIVITY 29

You've already looked for words that suggest a philosophical context. Now look for any other patterns – words or phrases that share a common context, repetitions, listing, word play by Lucky or the playwright, or anything that helps you to get a handle on the text. For every feature that you find, think how and where the same feature is present in the rest of the text. For instance, repetition occurs throughout the text in all sorts of ways.

Literary study

An interesting context for students of literature like yourselves is the context of literary study itself. This is a feature of *Educating Rita* which, after all, is concerned with Rita's efforts to be a student of literature. Look at this extract:

FRANK: You can't go. I want to talk to you about this. [*He gets her essay and shows it to her.*] Rita, what's this?

RITA: Is there something wrong with it?

FRANK: It's just, look, this passage about 'The Blossom' you seem to assume that the poem is about sexuality.

RITA: It is!

FRANK: Is it?

RITA: Well it's certainly like a richer poem, isn't it? If it's interpreted in that way.

FRANK: Richer? Why richer? We discussed it. The poem is a simple, uncomplicated piece about blossom, as if seen from a child's point of view.

RITA: [*shrugging*]: In one sense. But it's like, like the poem about the rose, isn't it? It becomes a more rewarding poem when you see that it works on a number of levels.

FRANK: Rita, 'The Blossom' is a simple uncomplicated . . .

RITA: Yeh, that's what you say, Frank; but Trish and me and some others were talkin' the other night, about Blake, an' what came out of our discussion was that apart from the simple surface value of Blake's poetry there's always a like erm – erm –

FRANK: Well? Go on . . .

RITA: [*managing to*]: – a like vein. Of concealed meaning. I mean that if that poem's only about the blossom then it's not much of a poem is it?

FRANK: So? You think it gains from being interpreted in this way?

RITA: [*slightly defiantly*]: Is me essay wrong then, Frank?

FRANK: It's not – not wrong. But I don't like it.

RITA: You're being subjective.

FRANK: [*half-laughing*]: Yes – yes I suppose I am. [*He goes slowly to the chair of the desk and sits down heavily.*]

RITA: If it was in an exam what sort of mark would it get?

FRANK: A good one.

RITA: Well what the hell are you sayin' then?

FRANK: [*shrugging*]: What I'm saying is that it's up to the minute, quite acceptable, trendy stuff about Blake; but there's nothing of you in there.

RITA: Or maybe Frank, y' mean there's nothing of your views in there.

FRANK: [*after a pause*]: Maybe that is what I mean?

RITA: But when I first came to you, Frank, you didn't give me any views. You let me find my own.

FRANK: [*gently*]: And your views I still value. But, Rita, these aren't your views.

RITA: But you told me not to have a view. You told me to be objective, to consult recognized authorities. Well that's what I've done; I've talked to other people, read other books an' after consultin' a wide variety of opinion I came up with those conclusions.

[*He looks at her.*]

Rita has clearly been taught about alternative interpretations of texts – Assessment Objective 4 in the AS syllabus ('it becomes a more rewarding poem when you see that it works on a number of levels'), and she compares the poem with another, 'The Sick Rose', in the context of the writer's other work (Assessment Objective 5i). She comments that 'there's always a like . . . a like vein. Of concealed meaning.'

Rita's 'Is me essay wrong then, Frank?' suggests that there is right and wrong. She probably knows that there isn't, so the remark is a challenge to Frank in literary terms, as is 'You're being subjective'. She has obviously made considerable progress in her efforts to become a literature student, but Frank puts his finger on the problem that has emerged: 'But, Rita, these aren't your views'. In other words, Rita has thought about different interpretations, and about contexts, but has yet to learn (or rather to relearn) what you will recognise as the first part of Assessment Objective 4 – the importance of giving 'informed, independent opinions and judgements'.

The language of this discussion is the language of literary study throughout – which is a measure in itself of the progress Rita has made, and how much she has changed. Recognising and understanding the context helps us to see this.

FRANK: For God's sake, why did you come back here?

RITA: I came to tell you you're a good teacher. [*After a pause.*] Thanks for enterin' me for the exam.

FRANK: That's all right. I know how much it had come to mean to you.

[RITA *perches on the small table while* FRANK *continues to take books from the upper shelves.*]

RITA: You didn't want me to take it, did y'? Eh? You woulda loved it if I'd written, 'Frank knows all the answers', across me paper, wouldn't y'? I nearly did an' all. When the invigilator said, 'Begin', I turned over me paper with the rest of them, and while they were all scribbling away against the clock, I just sat there, lookin' at the first question. Y' know what it was, Frank? 'Suggest ways in which one might cope with some of the staging difficulties in a production of *Peer Gynt*.' [FRANK *gets down, sits on the chair and continues to pack the books.*]

FRANK: Well, you should have had no trouble with that.

RITA: I did though. I just sat lookin' at the paper an' thinkin' about what you'd said. I tried to ignore it, to pretend that you were wrong. You think you gave me nothing; did nothing for me. You think I just ended up with a load of quotes an' empty phrases; an' I did. But that wasn't your doin'. I was so hungry. I wanted it all so much that I didn't want it to be questioned. I told y' I was stupid. It's like Trish, y' know me flatmate, I thought she was so cool an' together – I came home the other night an' she'd tried to top herself. Magic, isn't it? She spends half her life eatin' wholefoods an' health foods to make her live longer, an' the other half tryin' to kill herself. [*After a pause.*] I sat lookin' at the question, an' thinkin' about it all. Then I picked up me pen an' started.

FRANK: And you wrote, 'do it on the radio'?

RITA: I could have done. An' you'd have been proud of me if I'd done that an' rushed back to tell you – wouldn't y'? But I chose not to. I had a choice. I did the exam.

FRANK: I know. A good pass as well.

RITA: Yeh. An' it might be worthless in the end. But I had a choice. I chose, me. Because of what you'd given me I had a choice. I wanted to come back an' tell y' that. That y' a good teacher.

ACTIVITY 30

Here's another set of ideas and questions, this time to help you to see how a view of literary study is a constant in the text.

- The reference to the question on Peer Gynt reminds the audience of Rita's response to it earlier in the play. What was her original answer, and why wouldn't it have succeeded in the exam?

- Rita has moved on from her position in the previous extract, and is able to judge what she thought in her earlier state and why. Isolate the phrase that tells you what Rita's answer to the question might have been then – and that also tells you what would have been wrong with it.

- In terms of the skills she probably used, what do you think were the ingredients of Rita's answer once she'd decided to do the exam?

- What is it that has made Frank 'a good teacher', in Rita's view? What has he given her?

This section has taken you through a number of the contexts that might apply to your chosen texts, and given you some ideas about what to look for. Whichever play you're studying, look at the text carefully for all possible contexts – you won't know what contexts you'll be asked about in the examination.

You now know how you might identify and explore contexts – in the exam you have to write essays on contexts, which means drawing together what you've learned about the context of the text as a whole. Don't forget that you also have to demonstrate your skills in Assessment Objectives 1 and 2i, so you must communicate clearly (which means planning well, apart from anything else), use appropriate terminology, and write well. Your knowledge of contexts should reveal your understanding; but as in any literature essay, you must demonstrate your knowledge by giving evidence from the text to support your views.

Approaching the examinations

Revision

As the exams for your modules draw close, you will have to think about revision. Approach your revision in an organised and focused way. There are two important elements here: acquiring knowledge, and thinking about the Assessment Objectives for the questions on the paper.

Knowledge

Whatever you write on the set texts in the exams, you'll need to show your knowledge by using the text to support your views – quotations from the text, echoes of the texts, details of the text. There are no short cuts here, and no substitute for re-reading the text several times. After all, at each reading you don't simply remember more of the text; you also add to your store of understanding, as more and more of the way the text works is revealed to you. It's impossible to understand a text fully from one reading.

If you read your texts often enough, you'll have no problem in providing good support for what you want to say about the text in your exam response. There's no point in learning the 'best 15 quotations' – you don't know what the 'best' material is until you see the question. The evidence you should use is appropriate evidence.

The exam you take for Module 2 could well be the first time you've taken a closed book exam in English Literature. You might find this worrying – but you shouldn't. Having the text with you is only useful for 'open book' style questions that ask you to carefully re-examine some section of it. The text isn't there to provide knowledge – after all, you can't start reading the book in the exam, and you don't have time to start looking things up. You should know your texts by the time you take the exams, so closed book exams are nothing to fear.

The Assessment Objectives

This book, like the whole of your course, is based on the Assessment Objectives. It is not a good idea to forget about them when you come to the exam. The Assessment Objectives can guide your revision if you explore each text in relation to the Objectives that you'll be tested on. Of course, this means revisiting the work you've done in and outside class, but it provides a focus for your re-reading. For instance, for the drama text in Module 2i you'll be asked about contexts, so there's no point on spending much time in looking at the details of form, language and structure in the text unless one of these constitutes or provides evidence about a context. The reverse is true of the poetry text in the same paper.

Here's an exercise to help you revise the Assessment Objectives an how they should inform your approach to the examinations. The extract is from the play *The Steamie*, by Tony Roper. ('Steamies' were communal laundries in Glasgow.)

MAGRIT:	. . . Apart fae you dae mean?
ANDY:	Cause. [*Glasgow drunk's hand-signals.*] Zat's what ah'm here for . . . now then . . . z'ivrything awright?
MAGRIT:	[*this speech should be done with heavy irony to the audience as she sings 'Isn't it wonderful to be a woman'*]. Isn't it wonderful tae be a woman. Ye get up at the crack o' dawn and get the breakfast oan, get the weans ready and oot the hoose lookin' as tidy and as well dressed as ye can afford. Then ye see tae the lord high provider and get him oot, then wash up, finish the ironin', tidy the hoose and gie the flair a skite o'er. Then it's oot tae yer ain wee job, mebbe cleanin' offices, servin' in a shop or washin' stairs. Then it's dinner time. Well it is fur everyone else but no

us 'cause we don't get dinner. By the time yer oot and run home, cooked something for the weans, yer lucky if you feel like something tae eat. I know I don't and even if I did . . . the dinner hour's finished, so it's back tae yer work; that is efter ye've goat in whatever yer gonnae gie them for their tea, and efter yer finished yer work, ye'r back up . . . cookin' again and they'll tell ye the mince is lumpy . . . or the chips are too warm . . . then they're away oot. The weans tae play . . . the men tae have a drink, cause they need wan . . . the souls . . . efter pittin' in a hard day's graft, so ye've goat the hoose tae yersel' and what dae ye dae, ye tidy up again don't ye? Mer ironin, light the fire, wash the dishes and the pots etc. etc. and then ye sit doon. And what happens . . . ye've just sat doon when the weans come up. 'Gonnae make us a cuppa tea and something tae eat' . . . What dae ye's want tae eat? . . . 'Och anything Ma' . . . D'ye want some o' that soup? . . . 'Naw' . . . A tomato sandwich? . . . 'Naw' . . . A couple o' boiled eggs? . . . 'Naw' . . . A piece 'n spam? . . . 'Naw' . . . Well what d'ye's want? . . . 'Och anything at all'. So ye make them something tae eat then ye sit doon and finally have a wee blaw . . . a very wee blaw . . . cause it's time tae go tae the steamie. Ye go tae the steamie, finish at nine o'clock and get the washin' hame. Ye sort it aw oot . . . and get it put by and them sometimes mebbe take stock of yer life. What are we? . . . skivvies . . . unpaid skivvies . . . in other words we are . . . used . . . but ye think tae yersel', well even if I am being used . . . I don't mind . . . cause I love my family and anyway it's New Year's Eve. I can relax and jist enjoy masel . . . and any minute noo the weans'll be in an ma friends'll be comin' roon wi' black bun, shortbread, dumplin's, a wee refreshment and I can forget aw ma worries even if it's jist for a night and the weans arrive and ye gie them shortbread, sultana cake, ginger wine and there is just one thing missin', the head of the family. The door bell goes, ye open the door, and what is staunin there, ready to make the evening complete . . . that's right . . . your husband, your better half . . . the man who was goin' to make you the happiest woman in the world and [*Gently.*] what does he look like . . . *that.* [*At* ANDY.]

DOLLY:	Who were ye talkin' tae?
MAGRIT:	Masel.
ANDY:	So . . . z'a . . . wis sayin' girls . . . everything aw right doon here . . . know . . . cause . . . that's what I'm here fur.

What can you find in the passage that relates to Assessment Objectives 2–5? Remember that you need to provide evidence from the text for all your ideas. Here are some of the things you could think about:

- AO2i: *Type:* The extract is obviously from a play, but 'type' means more than **genre**. What type of play do you think it might be? Think about the period that the play appears to be set in, and the period when it was written – they might not be the same.

- AO3: *Form*: What is the effect of the stage directions? Who do you think Magrit's words are spoken to? This might make you speculate about the form of the whole play. *Language*: The language is obviously dialect, and the information given tells you it's Glasgow dialect. But there's a lot more to see. Think about the effect of the pronouns. Think about how humour is created, particularly with rhythm and repetition. Think about the tone – which words are obviously ironic? There's more, of course. *Structure*: The pronouns, and the form of the play, might make you think about the structure – of the passage here, and of the whole play. Look at the shape of Magrit's speech. How is it structured to finish the way it does?

- AO4: Two obvious readings of the text are Marxist and feminist. Look for evidence of both. Is this really a feminist piece? Look carefully at the end of Magrit's speech.

- AO5i: What different contexts can you find? Think about cultural, social, historical contexts, and the context of literary type and period.

In the examination

The most important thing in the exam room is to think and to plan. If you've studied and revised effectively you're full of knowledge, but it's easy to misuse this knowledge or present it ineffectively under the pressure of the exam. Here's what you should do:

Deconstruct the question. You know which Assessment Objectives are targeted, so look carefully for how they appear in the question and at exactly what you're asked to do. There's time allowed for thinking in the exam room. You've spent many hours reading your text over and over again, so you must certainly spare some minutes now to read through the question several times to make sure where the thrust of your response should be. Be careful. It can be dangerous when you think you 'recognise' a question – you probably don't; it just looks a bit like something you've thought about, and it's all too easy to set off on the wrong track.

Plan your response carefully. If you structure your responses carefully, in a logical progression, you'll be able to communicate your views clearly. Don't leave out this planning stage. All too often, candidates produce unstructured responses in the exam that don't really start delivering until halfway through. If you've planned clearly, you can spend your writing time following your plan and choosing the best words and the best evidence to support what you say as you go. (Remember that in Module 2 you have to answer two questions, and you should aim to split your time equally between the two.)

MODULE ③ Shakespeare

The Assessment Objectives for this module require that you:

ASSESSMENT OBJECTIVES

This module carries 30% of the total marks for the AS course. The marks are divided between the Assessment Objectives like this:

AO1 communicate clearly the knowledge, understanding and insight appropriate to literary study, using appropriate terminology and accurate and coherent written expression
(5% of the final AS mark; $2^1/_2$% of the final A Level mark)

AO2i respond with knowledge and understanding to literary texts of different types and periods
(5% of the final AS mark; $2^1/_2$% of the final A Level mark)

AO4 articulate independent opinions and judgements, informed by different interpretations of literary texts by other readers
(15% of the final AS mark; $7^1/_2$% of the final A Level mark)

AO5i show understanding of the contexts in which literary texts are written and understood
(5% of the final AS mark; $2^1/_2$% of the final A Level mark)

Shakespeare texts

You can choose any Shakespeare play or plays to study for this module, except:

- A play that you may subsequently choose in the 'Drama before 1770' section of Module 5 of the Advanced Level course, if you go on to complete it. One of the six plays in that section may be by Shakespeare; if you study this play as part of your AS coursework, you cannot then study it as an A Level text. For example, *Measure for Measure* is a choice in Module 5 in the 2002 A Level syllabus, so don't choose it for AS coursework if you're likely to study it at A Level.

- A play that you studied for Key Stage Three.

- A play that you studied for GCSE.

In other words, if you have written about a text in a previous examination or plan to study it at the next level, you should not choose it as your only text for this module. However, the syllabus states that you must study 'at least one' Shakespeare play. If you choose to write about two plays, *one* of these could be a play you'd studied before but not the other.

Coursework

This is a coursework module. You must study at least one play by Shakespeare, and write a coursework folder consisting of either two pieces of work of about 1,000 words each, or a single piece of work of about 2,000 words. You write the pieces at school or college or at home; then they are marked by your teacher. Finally, the Examination Board's moderator looks at all the work from your centre and decides on your final mark.

It's very important to choose appropriate tasks for your coursework – in other words, tasks that enable you to hit the Assessment Objectives for this module; keep them firmly in mind as you plan and write your work. Work with your teacher in choosing a task, and seek their guidance before handing in a final draft. Most of this chapter deals with the sorts of tasks you might choose for this module, and ways to tackle them. Here is some general advice about the production of coursework.

Producing coursework

Choosing a task

There are several things to think about here. You can undertake either one or two tasks in this module, and you must hit the Assessment Objectives. Whatever you do, you have to think about Assessment Objectives 1 and 2i as you write; but you need to choose tasks that deal with different interpretations (Assessment Objective 4) and contexts (Assessment Objective 5i) if you are going to do well. You could deal with these separately in two different tasks, but if you choose a single task you must make sure that your task includes both.

For instance, a critical analysis of a particular production you've seen, referring to other possible interpretations, could attract good marks under AO4 but few marks under AO5. Similarly, a detailed study of how the text was established may score well under AO5 but fail to attract many marks under AO4. But a detailed comparison of film and theatre versions of the play – particularly if these take different views of the text – could cover both Assessment Objectives in one piece. Remember too that AO4 asks you to 'articulate independent opinions and judgements', so your task should give you the opportunity to say what you think about the subject, bearing in mind the interpretations you've looked at.

Your task must be achievable too. If you decide to write a 1,000 word piece, there's no point in setting yourself a task that can't be done in less than 10,000 words. As a general rule, the more sharply defined the task, the better.

Reading the text

You'll probably read the text in class, where you'll have the chance to discuss it with your teacher and other students. But you'll need to read it again yourself too, just as you did when you prepared your exam texts. You must show 'knowledge and understanding' of the text (AO2i) in your writing, so the more you read it the better you'll know and understand it. This will enable you to focus on and use the text most effectively in supporting your interpretation, or in writing about contexts or other interpretations.

Planning and research

You must plan your piece or pieces. Bear in mind these three points:

- Your plan should be designed to help you write your piece, enabling you to develop your argument as a logical sequence of ideas that leads to a clear conclusion.

- Check your plan against the Assessment Objectives. Is it clear how and where you're going to achieve them?

- Think about length again. You don't want to have to make large changes to your plan once you start writing. Will the word total be about right by the time your plan is fleshed out with argument and evidence? If not, it's worth changing your plan now.

Your research may take you to articles or essays about your text, to books or the Internet, but the most important source is still the primary source: the text itself. For instance, if you decide to write about different interpretations of the female characters in *Hamlet*, you'd probably begin with a selective re-reading of the play, concentrating on Gertrude and Ophelia – what they say, what they do, the way other characters behave towards them. If you read secondary sources as part of your research, you must mention them in the bibliography at the end of your essay.

Writing

Ten of the 30 marks available for the Shakespeare module are for writing, and coursework offers a good chance to score well. Half of these 10 marks are for AO1, the ability to 'communicate clearly the knowledge, understanding and insight appropriate to literary study, using appropriate terminology and accurate and coherent written expression'. As long as you give yourself plenty of writing time, you can take more care over the accuracy and clarity of your writing than you can during an exam. You can take the time to check, revise and improve your writing when you've finished the first draft. There are specific marks for this, so it would be silly not to try to collect them.

The other five writing marks are for AO2i, the ability to 'respond with knowledge and understanding to literary texts'. The quality of your argument demonstrates your *understanding*; but your *knowledge* has to underpin everything you write, whether in coursework or examinations. Coursework gives you the leisure to practise what you have to do under time pressure in the exams – that is, to provide textual support for what you say. There are appropriate ways of showing knowledge too, by referring to details or echoes of the text or by quotation. Normally, you'll include short quotations (usually the most effective) in the body of your writing, whereas you can set out longer quotations on separate lines so that they're easier to read. If you quote lines of verse, show the line divisions. Here's an example of all these conventions at work in some writing about *The Winter's Tale*:

> Before the final moment, Paulina protests twice about the perception that any magic she might perform might be sinful: she refers to 'wicked powers' and 'unlawful business', recalling Prospero's firm 'no' when similarly accused in *The Tempest.* After the statue moves, Leontes is clear in her defence:
>
>> If this be magic, let it be an art
>> Lawful as eating.

If you're quoting from a secondary source, such as a critic, acknowledge this in a note by numbering the quotations and providing a guide to the numbers, either as a true footnote at the foot of the page or in a list of notes (endnotes) at the end of your piece. For instance:

> How literally should the audience take this moment? Bloom's view is that Paulina, while 'making reasonably clear that she is not a necromancer, is also careful to distance us from realism'.[1]
>
> This could be footnoted:
>
> [[1]Harold Bloom, *The Invention of the Human*, Fourth Estate, 1999, p. 660.]

If you use the words of other writers such as critics in your own writing, you must acknowledge them. You have to sign a declaration that the coursework is your own work. 'Lifting' from other writing without acknowledging it is called malpractice, and *may lose you all marks* for the module.

Drafting and redrafting

When you complete the first draft of your coursework piece, your teacher may allow you to redraft it – as long as there is enough time left. Your teacher is only allowed to give general advice and guidelines as to how you might improve the work, not to correct it or rewrite it – it must be your work, after all. Of course, you should heed any advice you get, but your first draft should be as good as you can make it. It's a lot easier to make minor changes than major ones.

Sticking to the word and time limits

The word limit for AS coursework is 2,000 words. If you exceed it, you run the risk of being penalised. It's as simple as that.

If your first draft comes to 2,400 words, you can probably trim it fairly easily. You may want your teacher's guidance concerning which parts to prune. But if it runs to 4,000 words, say, then you're in trouble – cutting sentences here and there and tightening expression won't cut the piece by 50%. Really, you made a mistake much earlier – when selecting the task, at the planning stage, or when you were part way through. That was the time to stop and think where you were going. Your teacher will give you coursework deadlines, and it's important to stick to them – not just to please your teacher, but to improve your chances of success. You will only be able to cut, redraft or rethink if you have the time to do it.

Coursework tasks

The following list of coursework tasks and ways of tackling them is by no means exhaustive. The tasks simply illustrate some ways of planning and writing successful coursework pieces, while keeping the Assessment Objectives firmly in focus. Reading through them may make you think of tasks you can tackle for your chosen text, or of completely different tasks that access the Objectives.

Part-to-whole context, and extending it

One valuable way of approaching context is to think about a particular passage from the play you're studying in relation to the whole play. Where does it belong in the dramatic and thematic structure of the play? How do the words and actions in the passage reverberate throughout the rest of the play? What is there in the language of the extract that has significance for the whole play?

As an example of how you might go about a task like this, here's Act 1 Scene 1 of *The Tempest*, followed by an activity that could lead to a coursework assignment.

> [*On a ship at sea: a tempestuous noise of thunder and lightning heard. Enter a* MASTER *and a* BOATSWAIN *severally*]
>
> MASTER: Boatswain!
> BOATSWAIN: Here master. What cheer?
> MASTER: Good. Speak to the mariners. Fall to't, yarely, or we run ourselves aground. Bestir, bestir.
> [*Exit*]
> [*Enter* MARINERS]
> BOATSWAIN: Heigh, my hearts! cheerly, cheerly, my hearts! yare, yare! Take in the topsail. Tend to the master's whistle. Blow, till thou burst thy wind, if room enough.

[*Enter* ALONSO, SEBASTIAN, ANTONIO, FERDINAND, GONZALO, *and others*]

ALONSO: Good boatswain have care. Where's the master? Play the men.

BOATSWAIN: I pray now keep below.

ALONSO: Where is the master, boatswain?

BOATSWAIN: Do you not hear him? You mar our labour. Keep your cabins: you do assist the storm.

GONZALO: Nay, good, be patient.

BOATSWAIN: When the sea is. Hence! What cares these roarers for the name of king? To cabin. Silence! Trouble us not.

GONZALO: Good, yet remember whom thou hast aboard.

BOATSWAIN: None that I more love than myself. You are a councillor; if you can command these elements to silence, and work the peace of the present, we will not hand a rope more. Use your authority. If you cannot, give thanks you have lived so long, and make yourself ready in your cabin for the mischance of the hour, if it so hap. Cheerly, good hearts! Out of our way I say. [*Exit*]

GONZALO: I have great comfort from this fellow. Methinks he hath no drowning mark upon him, his complexion is perfect gallows. Stand fast, good Fate, to his hanging; make the rope of his destiny our cable, for our own doth little advantage. If he be not born to be hanged, our case is miserable.

[*Exeunt*]
[*Re-enter* BOATSWAIN]

BOATSWAIN: Down with the topmast. Yare, lower; lower. Bring her to try with main-course. [*A cry within*] A plague upon this howling! They are louder than the weather or our office.

[*Re-enter* SEBASTIAN, ANTONIO, *and* GONZALO]

Yet again? What do you here? Shall we give o'er and drown? Have you a mind to sink?

SEBASTIAN: A pox o' your throat, you bawling, blasphemous, incharitable dog!

BOATSWAIN: Work you then.

ANTONIO: Hang, cur, hang, you whoreson, insolent noisemaker. We are less afraid to be drowned than thou art.

GONZALO: I'll warrant him for drowning, though the ship were no stronger than a nutshell, and as leaky as an unstanched wench.

BOATSWAIN: Lay her a-hold, a-hold; set her two courses off to sea again; lay her off.

[*Enter* MARINERS, *wet*]

MARINERS: All lost, to prayers, to prayers! All lost!
[*Exeunt*]

BOATSWAIN: What, must our mouths be cold?

GONZALO:	The King and Prince at prayers, let us assist them, for our case is as theirs.
SEBASTIAN:	I'm out of patience.
ANTONIO:	We are merely cheated of our lives by drunkards. This wide-chapped rascal – would thou might'st lie drowning The washing of ten tides!
GONZALO:	He'll be hanged yet, Though every drop of water swear against it. And gape at wid'st to glut him.
	[A confused noise within: 'Mercy on us!' – 'We split, we split!' – 'Farewell, my wife and children!' – 'Farewell, brother!' – 'We split, we split, we split!']
ANTONIO:	Let's all sink with the King. *[Exit]*
SEBASTIAN:	Let's take leave of him. *[Exit]*
GONZALO:	Now would I give a thousand furlongs of sea for an acre of barren ground, long heath, broom, furze, any thing. The wills above be done! but I would fain die a dry death. *[Exit]*

An interesting way to start thinking about the scene is to consider which words you would want the audience to hear if you were directing the play. This is a very real question: in a naturalistic staging of the first scene, it's likely that much of the dialogue will be drowned by the noise of the thunder and possibly of sea effects.

ACTIVITY 1

Working alone or in a group, identify which words are most important for the audience to hear and why. As you work, consider the following points:

- *Plot.* What do the audience need to know here that is important to an understanding of what happens later?

- *Character.* It's unlikely that the audience will make much of individual characters in this scene, but its impact suggests that something will be remembered. Which lines or actions say something significant about characters? Don't just think about individual characters. You could consider how the nobles and the seamen behave towards each other. Do all the noblemen behave in the same way? How do their words and actions foreshadow what we learn of them later?

- *Meanings.* Some words in this scene, or the ideas that they suggest, are found elsewhere in the play. For instance, not only is Gonzalo's exclamation 'The wills above be done!' typical of his attitude and character, but the idea of a controlling power beyond Prospero appears many times in the play – 'Heavens rain grace on that which breeds between 'em', for instance, in Act 2.

- *Language.* The scene is in prose, which is perhaps unsurprising given the frantic, disordered atmosphere that Shakespeare is creating here. But there are words that may have significance elsewhere in the play. For example, Sebastian remarks 'I'm out of patience', and the word 'patience' takes on a wider significance, particularly in the final scene, as shown in these lines:

ALONSO: Irreparable is the loss, and patience
           Says it is past her cure.
PROSPERO: I rather think
           You have not sought her help, of whose soft grace
           For the like loss I have her sovereign aid,
           And rest myself content.

Look for other examples of language that relate to the rest of the play.

Doing an exercise like this would provide you with the material to write a piece about Act 1 Scene 1 in the context of the play, drawing evidence from the passage and elsewhere in the play. Remember that you need to show knowledge and understanding of the play as well as write about contexts, so although this idea is based on the first scene you can see that you carry it through without knowledge and understanding of the whole play.

Another way of tackling part-to-whole context could be to find a single key line from a play, and show how it reverberates through the play in a number of ways.

ACTIVITY 2

Look at the line 'Are you our daughter?' from Act 1 Scene 4 of *King Lear*:

FOOL: . . . So out went the candle, and we were left darkling.
LEAR: Are you our daughter?
GONERIL: I would you would make use of your good wisdom, . . .

There are many ways of working from this line. Here are some suggestions:

- This is a significant moment in the plot. What does Lear start to realise that the audience already knows? Where does this lead?

- The question itself is significant. Who is Lear's true daughter, and in what sense?

- The corollary to 'Who are you?' is 'Who am I?' Does this moment start to reveal to Lear something about himself?

- What is happening to Lear's power here? Why is this significant in the whole play? Notice that Goneril's reply is not an answer to the question at all.

Lear is questioning what he can see in front of him with his own eyes – perhaps the beginning of him being able to 'see straight'. This obviously has a huge bearing on one of the meanings of the play, and its associated language, both in Lear's story and the blinding of Gloucester. How is the line 'I stumbled when I saw' relevant to this?

The choice of words is interesting, too, especially when compared with Lear's words in Act 4, when he wakes up from madness and recognises Cordelia: 'I think this lady / To be my child Cordelia'. Notice that every word from 'Are you our daughter?' has changed: 'our' has become 'my', 'daughter' has become 'child', and so on. Why? What does it tell you about Lear's state of mind, and his change?

'Are you our daughter?' is a half line of verse – the line is incomplete; Goneril's response forms a new line. What happens in the pause that is created? Who is the audience looking at? What might Lear be thinking?

If you don't know *King Lear* you won't have been able to do all of Activity 2, but the questions should have given you some idea of the features to look for.

ACTIVITY 3

In your chosen play, look for a line that resonates through the text like the one from *King Lear*, so that you can open up a number of aspects of the play. Choose a line that is significant in some of these aspects of the play: plot; character and relationships; meanings; form, structure and language; action.

Remember that your aim is to write about the line in relation to the rest of the play – the *context* – and to show *knowledge* and *understanding*, offering a range of aspects and sufficient evidence at each step.

Extending the piece: interpretations

A piece written in this way about the first scene of *The Tempest* or an extract from any of Shakespeare's plays would gain marks for the context requirement, but not the 15 available marks for interpretations. This means it would have to be one of two 1,000 word pieces; you'd have to write another 1,000 word study aimed specifically at interpretations.

You could, however, look for ways in which this kind of piece could be extended to include AO4. For instance, you could suggest alternative ways in which the *Tempest* scene could be staged, clearly tied to different interpretations of the play. This could extend to include the beginning of the next scene, where interpretations might be clear in such elements as the nature of the 'magic' at work, the power relationship between Miranda and Prospero, or Prospero's treatment of Ariel and Caliban.

As long as your plan carefully integrates the two strands into a coherent single piece, this combined approach would satisfy all the Assessment Objectives for the module in a single 2,000 word piece.

Critical analysis of a particular production with reference to other possible interpretations

This might well be a popular choice for a number of candidates – after all, the best way to understand the plays as theatre is to see and hear them in the environment for which they were written. You should always seize the chance to see a production of a play you're studying if you can, so why not make it the basis of a coursework piece?

If this looks like an easy option, think again. It would be very easy to write a piece that simply described the production – and it wouldn't get you very far. Remember that the key Assessment Objectives you must address in this module are to 'articulate independent opinions and judgements, informed by different interpretations of literary texts by other readers', and to 'show understanding of the contexts in which literary texts are written and understood'.

You have to show evidence of these Objectives in your writing, so they have to be in your head when you see the production. You must have a firm idea of what you're looking for (see below). Jot down your thoughts and ideas as soon as possible after you've seen the play – rather than attempt this during the play, when there's so much to see and hear. It's even better if you can see a production more than once, to build on what you saw the first time.

To see how this might work, look at the following examples.

Macbeth

A recent production of *Macbeth* had these key features of presentation:

- Lady Macbeth was shown as pregnant. This was clear from her first appearance and became more pronounced, so the signs of a miscarriage were evident in the sleepwalking scene.

- The witches were on stage for most of the action, because they played all the parts without names, and Seyton, as well as their own.

These features might have led you to notice several other things:

Presentation of character. Lady Macbeth's pregnancy made her seem even more callous at times: 'I would . . . Have plucked my nipple from his boneless gums / And dashed the brains out' seemed more real and more chilling from a pregnant woman. The blood on her legs in the sleepwalking scene, though horrible, made sense of her suicide and madness. The relationship between the Macbeths achieved an unusual sort of intimacy, and affected the physicality between them. When Macbeth was broken by his wife in Act 1 Scene 7, he fell to his knees and was pulled in to the visibly pregnant stomach on 'We fail?', suggesting a different sort of sexual relationship and control to the one usually chosen.

The witches' presence on stage kept them at the centre of the action, observing and prompting. They became more controlling and omniscient.

Management of plot/action. The witches' role here was crucial. They became part of the action, not separate from it. For instance, the play began with all the male characters on stage, ready for Act 1 Scene 2. The witches (two played by men, one by a woman) were dressed as part of the army, and were picked out by lighting for the opening lines. They brought down the lights for the interval, too. And at the end of the play, as soldiers again, they were left on stage with Macbeth's head and sword when Malcolm's army departed.

Dramatic structure. This idea for the ending altered the play's structure. The play was now begun and ended by the witches, which again emphasised their control.

Thematic issues. Lady Macbeth's pregnancy had a bearing on the theme of children in the play. It gave force to Macbeth's concern about the 'barren sceptre' placed in his hand, 'no son of mine succeeding', and his horror at the vision of Banquo's crowned descendants. The vision of the 'bloody child' might mean Macduff – but the tragic culmination of the pregnancy produced another meaning.

The greatest effect on the play's meaning came from the presentation of the witches. Because they watched over Macbeth all the time and prompted him to some extent – throwing the dagger on to the stage for him to find, for instance – they seemed to have more control, and therefore took some of the responsibility for his evil deeds from him. This was particularly clear in Act 5. The decision to use the witches for all the unnamed characters meant that Macbeth was surrounded by witches in his castle – even when everybody else had left. This created more sympathy for him, perhaps, but altered the nature of the play.

Writing the assignment

Seeing and hearing these sorts of features will help you to write a critical analysis of the production, and to address the first part of AO4 – to 'articulate independent opinions and judgements'. You can start to work on the second part – 'informed by different interpretations of literary texts by other readers' – by measuring what you saw against your own interpretation of the play, perhaps beginning with your own prior expectations. But you must do more for a really full response. Bearing in mind the thrust of this particular production, you could produce critical writing about issues like this:

- Lady Macbeth in relation to children; should she be seen as barren?

- the role of the witches in the play

- the extent of Macbeth's responsibility for his own downfall.

If you then measure such views against what you saw and come to your own evaluation of its merits, you would satisfy all the elements of AO4. But this time there's nothing about contexts, so this type of assignment would have to be one of two 1,000 word pieces on the play. Remember: if you decide to write one assignment of 2,000 words it has to address both Objectives.

Hamlet

A recent RSC production of *Hamlet* had these key features:

- The text was heavily cut, losing most of the 'political', public elements.

- The costume was largely modern dress; and there were a number of clearly 'modern' cultural references – Ophelia's drug habit, for instance.

As in the case of *Macbeth*, these production features might have led you to notice several other things:

Presentation of character. The main effect of cutting the text, apart from the playing length, was to make the play far more personal – a much more intense study of Hamlet's psychology. This was further pointed up by a video clip used at both the beginning and end of the play, showing a boy playing in the snow with his father; its final moment showed the boy running to his father's arms. Again, Hamlet's psychology and a Freudian interpretation of the play bracketed its action.

Management of plot/action. The location of action was also changed along with the text. The first scene of the play was replaced by one that placed Hamlet alone with his father's ashes. Scene 2 was presented as a party for Claudius and Gertrude, where Hamlet was brought news of the Ghost, and the Ghost appeared. Again, this produced both fluency of movement from scene to scene and a sense of compacted action.

Dramatic structure. The dramatic structure was clearly altered. Beginning and ending the play with Hamlet and his father created a quite different emphasis that centred on this pairing. There was no need for Fortinbras because the political elements had gone, and the play ended, as far as the text went, with Hamlet's death, before the final clip was shown.

Performance and staging. The interpretation of the play, and the cutting decisions, threw more weight than ever on the actor playing Hamlet, not simply in his semi-permanence on stage, but in the portrayal of grief and its effects. The modern setting was played to the full, with dramatic lighting for the party scenes and soliloquies, and the set dominated by a huge, shadowy statue of the former King placed upstage – again, in line with the interpretation.

Writing the assignment

As with the first example, seeing and hearing these features of the production will help you to write a critical analysis of the production, and to address the 'opinion and judgement' part of AO4. Similarly, you can work towards the 'interpretation' component by measuring what you saw against your own interpretation of the play, perhaps beginning from your own expectations. This time your critical writing could concentrate on issues such as:

- the Ghost, and its influence on Hamlet

- Hamlet's psychology, particularly from a Freudian viewpoint.

To satisfy all the requirements of AO4, measure these views against what you saw and then come to your own evaluation of its merits. However, if you're doing a single 2,000 word piece on this play, you must also incorporate AO5 and write about contexts. Here are some possible contextual issues that you could research and think about for this production:

- The political situations and theories that might have interested Shakespeare and his audience when he wrote the play. For instance, there was no obvious heir to the throne and there was much speculation as to who would succeed Elizabeth, leading to the activities of the Cecils and other complicated political manoeuvrings behind the scenes. This can be seen at work in the play several times. A contemporary audience would have been well aware that Hamlet's chosen successor Fortinbras was from a country to the north of Denmark – as Scotland is to England.

- How the altered key scenes might have been presented in the early performances.

You could then go on to consider whether the loss of the political scenes is important for a modern audience, and to what extent the interpretation depended on modern staging techniques. This approach would satisfy the requirements of AO5, so you would have met both key Objectives in a single piece.

Comparison of different productions

Attending a performance

When you attend a play with a view to writing about it as a piece of coursework, you must be organised to get the best out of your visit.

Before you go
You're presumably already familiar with the play. If you haven't looked at it for a while, remind yourself of it and think about what you expect to see and hear on the stage. Remember that what you eventually write must relate to the key Objectives AO4 and AO5i.

At the performance
Don't jot things down during the performance – your eyes and ears should be on the stage. If you decide to write something down, keep it very brief and make sense of it afterwards; you could use the interval if there is one. Here are some of the things you should look for as you watch:

Interpretations. Try to find evidence of ideas that inform the production and reveal how the director and cast want the audience to see the play. Look for clues in:

- the presentation of characters and relationships

- the management of the plot and action, and whether there are cuts or changes in sequencing

- the set: whether it is representational, and/or what it suggests

- the period suggested by the set, and whether that has a bearing on what the audience think about the action

- the costume and props: do they assist the interpretation?

Contexts. Looking at the set, costume and props together should begin to reveal contexts. You probably know something about the society, politics and theatre of Shakespeare's time – some of the cultural and historical contexts of the first performance of the play. There are already two contexts at work here, as a modern audience in a modern theatre looks at the play differently. If the play is set in a different period from that of the original performances, this creates another context that may make the audience think differently about the ideas in the play. The new context may be reflected in the way the actors relate to each other in movement and speech, as well as in the more obvious 'dressing' of costume, set and props.

After the performance

Unless you're going to start writing your assignment straight away, now is the time to make notes while the performance is still fresh in your mind. Think about the list of issues above and anything else that struck you about the production. If others saw the play with you, it's helpful to discuss your thoughts now – they may have spotted things that you missed, or perhaps saw the production differently. Read reviews of the production if they are available; after all, these are interpretations too – and different reviews may reveal alternative attitudes to the text or the performance.

Practising your skills

You may not be able to see another play before you see the one you're going to write about, but if you do you could practise this process. Or you could try out some of the techniques on a TV drama, or a film version of the play you're studying.

If you have the opportunity to see two different productions of a play, this could form an excellent basis for a piece centring on interpretations. After all, there are three interpretations open to you immediately – those of the two productions, and your own view. AO4 requires you to 'articulate independent opinions and judgements, informed by different interpretations of literary texts by other readers'. Balancing the two interpretations, with evidence, and arguing your own view of the play in relation to them, with evidence that shows knowledge and understanding, meets the requirements of Objectives 2i and 4. Here's how you might go about it.

The second production

Before you go
Your preparation for the second production will be similar to your preparation for the first. However, this time you should carefully review your thoughts on the interpretations offered by the first production.

At the performance
Although you will be looking for much the same things as you did at the first production, you now have something else to focus on: the similarities and differences between the two productions. And remember, the differences you're looking for are not simply the surface features – the age and appearance of the actors, the sets, costume, props, effects and so on. You are trying to determine what all these elements taken together suggest to the audience about the play and its meanings.

After the performance
Again, your thinking and discussion should centre on comparing this production with the first, and particularly on differences in interpretation.

Writing the assignment

Here you're focusing on comparing the two productions and the interpretations they offered, so your plan should reflect this. You also need to give your own view of the productions and the play. Here are four possible ways to approach your planning:

- an analysis of production 1; an analysis of production 2; comparison/ contrast of the two productions; your view

- an analysis of production 1; an analysis of production 2, comparing and contrasting as you go; your view

- an analysis of productions 1 and 2 together, comparing and contrasting features as you go; your view

- an introduction, using your overview, of both text and productions; an analysis of productions 1 and 2 together, comparing and contrasting features as you go and using your views as indicators; and a conclusion that evaluates the comparative success of the productions.

Any of these approaches could succeed. Remember that in writing the piece you must show knowledge as well as understanding, by using details not only from the productions but from the text or texts.

Comparison of film and theatre versions

This choice certainly gives you the opportunity to meet both of the important Objectives for this module, AO4 and AO5i. To meet them both successfully, the versions you look at need to offer different interpretations, and a film version must be more than simply a stage performance recorded on film. This is to enable you to write about the separate contexts of stage and film.

Examples of choices

If you were studying *The Tempest* and had the chance to see a stage production of the play, there are several film versions available on video that you could study alongside the production.

- The BBC version, with Michael Hordern, offers a fairly conventional reading of the play, with settings quite close to a stage set. At the same time, however, the androgynous representation of Ariel and the attitudes of Prospero offer material for discussion of interpretations. The filming of the opening and the appearances of Ariel and the other spirits would lead to discussion of contexts.

- More unconventional are Derek Jarman's 1980 filmed version, and Peter Greenaway's *Prospero's Books* (1991). Both films treat the play in quite startling ways, and offer much to discuss and write about in terms of interpretations and context. For example, you could look at one of these two versions, the Hordern version, and a stage production.

There are several film versions of *Macbeth* available too. Roman Polanski's 1972 film and the recording of the RSC studio production with Ian McKellen and Judi Dench are quite different, and offer strong interpretations of the relationships between characters. Comparing either or both of these with a stage production would be a viable option.

Kurosawa's *Ran*, his film of *King Lear*, offers an excellent basis for a comparison with a stage production – not only in some unusual interpretations, but also for the Japanese context that the director uses so cleverly to affect the audience's view of the play.

Watching a film to compare with a stage version

Much of your attention will be on the same elements as in a stage production (see the boxes above). Interpretations, and the ways that characters' relationships, setting, costume, etc. develop them, will still be high on your agenda. But there are other elements that are peculiar to film. Here are some things to think about:

Use of setting/place. Film offers greater opportunities than the stage for using a variety of settings and locations. Has this been done, and what effect do the places have on the view of the play that is offered?

Lighting/colour. Because of the nature of the medium, the production can concentrate on particular colours or use lighting effects peculiar to cinema. What do you notice, and why are these colours/effects being used?

Camera distance and angle. Apart from promenade productions, the angle of the audience member to the stage doesn't alter much. But film productions

---

can use long and short shots, close-ups, panning and tracking shots, and a variety of angles. Look for camera techniques that clearly enhance a particular moment or line in the play.

Cutting/fading. Film offers a number of techniques for moving from scene to scene, or moment to moment, that are not open to a stage director. Techniques like cutting and fading might have been used not simply to speed the action, but to create an effect – perhaps by juxtaposing sharply one moment, event or character against another. Again, it's these purposes you should be looking for once you've seen the technique.

Music/sound. Of course, music and sound may well be used in the stage production that you see, but music and sound effects are often used more extensively in film. If this is so, what effects do they achieve? Try to be as exact as you can.

Special effects. A play with 'magic' elements, such as *Macbeth, The Tempest* or *A Midsummer Night's Dream*, might well be filmed using special film effects. And film techniques such as split-screen shots could be used for any filmed play. Why, exactly, have any of these techniques been used?

Soliloquies. A feature of most of the Shakespeare plays that you are likely to study is the soliloquy – a speech made by a character when alone on the stage that allows the audience to see and hear the character's thoughts. How have these passages been delivered in the film?

Writing the assignment

The danger in writing about a film version of a play you're studying is that you are tempted to write about the film only as a film. There's no point in writing about any of the above techniques without relating them to *purpose* – the director's purposes in making the audience see the play in a particular way. It's the *play* that must be at the centre of your discussion – this is an English Literature course, not a film course.

Your plan for the assignment might well look like one of the plans in the last section, comparing one production to another. If you're doing one 2,000 word piece, remember that you must meet all the Assessment Objectives in the module; you'll need to write about contexts as well as interpretations when you're comparing the versions you saw. And you must use evidence to support your views of the play in its several versions, to show your knowledge and understanding.

Proposals for staging the text, with alternative possibilities

This is an attractive option, in that it allows you to think about the play both practically and creatively. There are some dangers, though. Your piece obviously addresses AO4, the 'interpretations' Objective, so you must ensure that what you write is aimed directly at this. There would be no point in writing about costume, setting, stage action or any other feature of staging without relating them to your interpretation of the play. You should also suggest some alternative stagings, linked to other interpretations, to meet the whole Objective. You must show 'knowledge and understanding', too, so your suggestions need to be referenced in the text.

Another danger of this choice is writing too much. You're not trying to write a full production script, working through the play chronologically: the outcome would inevitably be long and repetitive. You're concerned with the principles of staging your interpretation and others – the different production elements should be framed in this context. You'll probably want to consider key scenes or moments from the play, particularly those that are quite different in the various interpretations you offer.

Example

In the second suggestion for coursework, on pages 121–22 above, the example on *Macbeth* featured a particular interpretation of the witches. If you had come up with this idea, you can see that your interpretation would have required the following staging elements:

- *How the players were dressed.* They would have to be in a variety of costumes to suit the parts they played, such as soldiers, waiting gentlewoman, and so on.

- *The gender of the players.* In this production there was one female witch and two males, one white and one black. This in itself offered a variety of role playing.

- *How the players behaved.* Their degree of control was indicated by the way they seemed to command the lighting, and the throwing of the dagger into the stage for Macbeth to find.

- *The management of the action.* This would be very noticeable to the audience, because the witches closed both acts of the play.

- *The effects on stage of their presentation.* In Act 5 they surrounded Macbeth, and stage positioning would emphasise this. This in turn, together with the other elements above, would suggest an interpretation of Macbeth – that his responsibility for his evil deeds was lessened by their evident control.

A different staging possibility would depend on an alternative interpretation of the same element or elements of the play, so you would think of something different to do with the witches – and the reason for it. An obvious possibility is a traditional 'witchy' presentation using elderly females with black hats, broomsticks and cauldrons – but you must think in terms of how this could shape an alternative interpretation for the audience.

Another possibility might be to make the witches 'inner voices' for Macbeth, and for Banquo too the first time. The interpretation would be quite different in effect: clearly the responsibility for his actions would lie more heavily with Macbeth than in either of the other possibilities. So how would you stage it?

A simple voice-over using microphones would probably be theatrically deadening for an audience. Here are some other aspects to think about:

How they are dressed. One unchanged costume is presumably right here – they are apparently unseen anyway, so changes in appearance might be confusing. 'Blacks' might be obvious, or something deliberately anonymous, or even no clothes at all (if you like that sort of thing), to suggest the naked desires that the witches effectively represent.

Their gender. Presumably male only here, to echo male inner thought – unless a deliberate tie with Lady Macbeth is sought, which might also be reflected in costume. You could even use just one witch to match the interpretation, with perhaps a second for Banquo.

Behaviour/stage action. The obvious way to suggest their role is to have them always out of Macbeth's eyeline, perhaps behind him and whispering in his ear. Could Lady Macbeth do the same at some point? Clearly this might be varied once they were established. Particular moments could be studied – how would you do the first scene, for instance? Would Macbeth be present, but silent? The second scene with the witches would be interesting to design; two characters 'see' them, and the apparitions could be looked at too. It might be interesting to have them appear silently somewhere in Act 5 – an effect that would be quite different from that created by the omnipresent witches in the first interpretation.

Delivery of lines/emphasis. The witches' lines could be less coloured vocally, or whispered, to underline their function here – at least initially, until the idea is grounded with the audience.

The effects on stage of their presentation. Clearly, the likely predominant staging position, with the witches behind Macbeth, pushes him out towards the audience. This allows the audience a better sight of his responses to the inner voices, which would assist with the intention.

Working out the staging possibilities

You need to find an aspect of your text that could be played in a number of ways, to suggest different interpretations. For each possible interpretation, you must think about how it would be shown, which in turn depends on the play and what you're doing with it. Think in terms of the following range of staging elements.

The *colour of costumes* might be significant, to suggest character, or what the character represents. Obviously, period can be significant too: different historical contexts, which might suggest different readings of the text, can be suggested by costume, probably in conjunction with set and props.

Given *male characters don't necessarily have to be played by men*, or women by women. Shakespeare's women were played by boys, and in recent times several leading male parts have been played by women, with particular effects – Fiona Shaw has played Richard II, for instance, and Kathryn Hunter has played King Lear.

How the character is played might be very significant. Think in terms of how the actors behave and speak the lines, and what they choose to emphasise – but remember that whatever you say needs linking to your intentions, to the interpretation. The witches' whispering suggested above, for instance, is not just to make them sound sinister – it's to suggest that they should be seen as inner voices of Macbeth. Your suggested interpretation could lead you to ask that the actors pick out particular words or phrases.

In the same way, it is only valuable to comment on stage action and stage positioning if you can link them successfully to interpretation. It's how the audience sees them that's important.

It's a good idea to show these staging elements, or some of them, working at particular moments in a scene or part of a scene where this staging and interpretation are particularly clear.

Writing the assignment

Because this assignment is targeted at AO4, the 'interpretations' Objective, it's important to frame all your staging suggestions in the light of interpretation. This begins at the thinking stage, and continues with planning. You need to begin with the interpretation that shapes the staging, and make sure that other staging possibilities are firmly rooted in other interpretations.

You must also show 'knowledge and understanding', of course, so your suggestions should use the text, and show a considered and supported view of what it might mean. Your evaluation – your independent opinion and judgement, in other words – whether integrated into the piece or delivered as a conclusion, should weigh the interpretations and/or the staging possibilities against each other.

Extending the piece: adding contexts

A thorough attempt at this sort of assignment could well take you beyond 1,000 words, even if you write concisely, so you may prefer to add a discussion of context and extend your piece to a 2,000 word assignment that covers all the Assessment Objectives. One context you could consider here is that of the stage itself – staging as opposed to reading, or the stage in Shakespeare's theatre and now, or different types of staging space. You could find an interpretation that is particularly suited to a stage in the round, which would affect your staging suggestions.

Offering an interpretation, with alternative views

A straightforward way of tackling AO4 is to look at a particular aspect of the text you're studying and give your reading of it – taking into account other views of this aspect, either from different critical standpoints or from critics who have expressed a view.

It's not enough to have an interesting idea about the text that is simply at variance with other ideas. You must argue your interpretation with evidence that can show your knowledge and understanding. Once you've started to think about an interpretation, the essential first step is to gather evidence from the text.

Gathering evidence from the text

Let's suppose that you decide to write about the women in *Hamlet* and choose to show that they are surprisingly frail in character. Here's some of the evidence you might use – it's up to you to decide how to use it to make your case.

Gertrude

- Hamlet says that she 'would hang on him / As if increase of appetite had grown / By what it fed on.' He says that she 'posts with such dexterity to incestuous sheets'.

- The Ghost says that Claudius 'won to his shameful lust / The will of my most seeming virtuous Queen'; and 'so lust, though to a radiant angel link'd / Will sat itself in a celestial bed / And prey on garbage.' He describes the throne of Denmark as 'a couch for luxury and damned incest'.

A clear picture of this woman appears in these lines. Of course, the views of the two characters who say the lines may be biased, but she does remarry very quickly.

- Look at her own words. When she considers the Player Queen, she doesn't regard her as honest, but rather cynically: 'The lady doth protest too much, methinks'. When she thinks about Ophelia's death, her thoughts move quickly to the marriage bed: 'I hop'd thou should'st have been my Hamlet's wife: / I thought thy bride-bed to have deck'd . . .'

- What about her behaviour towards her son? Her first words to him in the play tell him to forget his father: 'do not for ever . . . seek for thy noble father in the dust'.

She goes along with the use of Rosencrantz and Guildenstern, the Claudius/Polonius plot to watch him with Ophelia to see how he behaves, and the introduction of a spy into her bedchamber. She allows Polonius to tell her how to behave. Claudius is sure that she will not be an obstacle in the plan to murder Hamlet (Act 4 Scene 7).

Ophelia

- Look at her words: 'I do not know, my lord, what I should think'. She is instructed by her father not to talk to Hamlet: 'I shall obey, my lord'; 'I did repel his letters, and denied his access to me'. 'This in obedience hath my daughter shown me', says Polonius.

- Look at her behaviour. Like Gertrude, she goes along with the plot to discover the source of Hamlet's madness, allowing herself to be used in it. She returns her 'remembrances' to Hamlet, so that Claudius and Polonius can see the effect. How much does she love him?

- She says of herself that she is 'of ladies most deject and wretched', and 'Oh woe is me!' Who is she sorry for?

Having selected this evidence, you could make a case that shows both of these women as weak and morally suspect. To demonstrate your understanding, though, you need to look for the apparent flaws in your case and then try to fit them to your interpretation. The obvious problem is the audience's impression of the two women, especially in the light of Ophelia's madness and death and Gertrude's report of it. What can you say that will anticipate these objections?

- Look at the scene where Hamlet jumps into Ophelia's grave. Once he's done so, how much does he say about his feelings for Ophelia?

- Look carefully at the report of Ophelia's death in Act 4 Scene 7. Was her death a deliberate act?

- Shakespeare presents Gertrude very favourably here, quite deliberately. He gives the report of the death to her, though anybody could have delivered it. The speech is full of pathos and beautiful imagery, a deliberate choice that affects the way the audience thinks about Ophelia and Gertrude. The dialogue and verse are manipulated so that the account ends with Gertrude saying 'drown'd, drown'd', the only two words on the line. What is the audience looking at and thinking in the pause created before the next line?

Does all this undermine your earlier argument? What was Shakespeare doing with this scene? Perhaps if we feel more sympathetic towards her, this helps to accentuate the tragedy of Hamlet's loss when she dies and the treachery of Claudius. But you could argue that this doesn't change her earlier behaviour.

Although you would have formed an interpretation by using the evidence above, to fulfil the terms of the Assessment Objective you need to look at 'different interpretations of literary texts by other readers'. Within a feminist view of the women, you could examine the way that they are both exploited, manipulated and used by the men in the play – not excluding Hamlet, of course, in his treatment of Ophelia. Or you could easily find a more traditional view of both women that sees them as something akin to tragic heroines. You must produce evidence for these claims too.

Writing the assignment

You must plan this piece carefully, just as you did when you compared productions (see page 126). There are a number of ways to go about this, but to meet the Objectives you must be sure that your 'independent opinion' is balanced by other interpretations of the text, so that you can offer a 'judgement' based on these readings. Again, as in the suggested plans for comparing productions, you can either deal with different readings separately or integrate them into your own angle as you go – but to succeed you must produce a clear evaluation at the end. The quality and effectiveness of your evidence will determine how well you match up to the requirements that your opinions are 'informed' and that you show 'knowledge and understanding'.

Extending the piece: adding contexts

The type of piece outlined above is clearly a 1,000 word example aimed at AO4, and would have to be matched by a separate piece including contexts (AO5) to complete your file. But perhaps the thrust of this piece could be extended to include consideration of some contexts, which would allow you to submit one piece of 2,000 words.

In the example above, for instance, you could look at the expectations of women, and their relationships with men, in Shakespeare's society. This clearly provides a context, but you must remember to relate it to the women and men in the text – how they mirror that society, or even challenge it. It's how the context affects your reading of the text that matters. You could also look at the presentation of women in other Shakespeare plays, which are very different, on the whole – the module requirement states that you must study *at least* one play by Shakespeare, not *only* one play. This discussion could also develop your view about another context, that of Shakespeare's writing as a whole. Is this kind of extension possible with the play that you're studying?

Dealing with a conceptual context

Shakespeare's plays reveal a number of concerns that he returns to again and again in a number of plays. These effectively create a context – each one is an element that affects our reading of the play. Where does it appear? How? What emerges about this concept in this particular play or plays, or in these particular speeches or scenes? Here are some of the conceptual contexts to look for:

- kingship

- justice

- appearance and reality

- time

- fate

- redemption

- the nature of tragedy

- the nature of love.

Example

If you have been studying either *King Henry IV, Part 2* or *King Henry V*, you could read the other (remember that the requirement is at least one play – more are fine), and look at the ideas about kingship expressed in the plays. 'Expressed', of course, doesn't just mean what people say; it's what they do, too – and a play can express an idea through a number of different characters and situations.

Here are two key passages from the plays, in this context. First, two from *Henry IV, Part 2:*

KING HENRY: How many thousand of my poorest subjects
Are at this hour asleep! O sleep, O gentle sleep!
Nature's soft nurse, how have I frighted thee,
That thou no more wilt weigh my eyelids down
And steep my senses in forgetfulness?
Why rather, sleep, liest thou in smoky cribs,
Upon uneasy pallets stretching thee
And hush'd with buzzing night-flies to thy slumber,
Than in the perfumed chambers of the great,
Under the canopies of costly state,
And lull'd with sound of sweetest melody?
O thou dull god, why liest thou with the vile
In loathsome beds, and leav'st the kingly couch
A watch-case or a common 'larum-bell?
Wilt thou upon the high and giddy mast
Seal up the ship-boy's eyes, and rock his brains
In cradle of the rude imperious surge,
And in the visitation of the winds,
Who take the ruffian billows by the top,
Curling their monstrous heads and hanging them
With deaf'ning clamour in the slippery clouds,
That, with the hurly, death itself awakes?
Canst thou, O partial sleep! give thy repose
To the wet sea-boy in an hour so rude,
And in the calmest and most stillest night,
With all appliances and means to boot,
Deny it to a king? Then happy low, lie down!
Uneasy lies the head that wears a crown.

What difference does Henry distinguish between himself and his subjects? In the next extract, Hal sees his father's crown on his pillow. Look at the nouns and adjectives used about the crown. What picture emerges of kingship? What does the crown do to the wearer?

HAL: No; I will sit and watch here by the king.

         [*Exeunt all but HAL*]

         Why doth the crown lie there upon his pillow,
         Being so troublesome a bedfellow?
         O polish'd perturbation! golden care!
         That keep'st the ports of slumber open wide
         To many a watchful night! Sleep with it now!
         Yet not so sound, and half so deeply sweet
         As he whose brow with homely biggin bound
         Snores out the watch of night. O majesty!
         When thou dost pinch thy bearer, thou dost sit
         Like a rich armour worn in heat of day,
         That scalds with safety. . . .

The next two extracts are from *Henry V*. Hal, now King, visits his troops in disguise the night before the battle of Agincourt and discusses the responsibilities of the king with some of his men.

HAL: I dare say you love him not so ill to wish him here alone, howsoever you speak this to feel other men's minds. Methinks I could not die anywhere so contented as in the King's company, his cause being just and his quarrel honourable.

WILLIAMS: That's more than we know.

BATES: Ay, or more than we should seek after, for we know enough, if we know we are the King's subjects. If his cause be wrong, our obedience to the King wipes the crime of it out of us.

WILLIAMS: But if the cause be not good, the King himself hath a heavy reckoning to make; when all those legs and arms and heads, chopped off in battle, shall join together at the latter day, and cry all 'We died at such a place', some swearing, some crying for a surgeon, some upon their wives left poor behind them, some upon the debts they owe, some upon their children rawly left. I am afeard there are few die well that die in a battle, for how can they charitably dispose of any thing when blood is their argument? Now, if these men do not die well, it will be a black matter for the King that led them to it, whom to disobey were against all proportion of subjection.

HAL: So, if a son that is by his father sent about merchandise do sinfully miscarry upon the sea, the imputation of his wickedness, by your rule, should be imposed upon his father that sent him; or if a servant, under his master's command transporting a sum of money, be assailed by robbers and die in many irreconciled iniquities, you may call the business of the master the author of the servant's damnation. But this is not so: the King is not bound to answer the particular endings of his soldiers, the father of his son, nor the master of his servant; for they purpose not their death when they purpose their services. Besides, there is no king, be his cause never so spotless, if it come to the arbitrement of swords, can try it out with all unspotted soldiers. Some, peradventure, have on them the guilt of premeditated and contrived murder, some, of beguiling virgins with the broken seals of perjury, some, making the wars their bulwark, that have before gored the gentle bosom of peace with pillage and robbery. Now, if these men have defeated the law and outrun native punishment, though they can outstrip men, they have no wings to fly from God. War is his beadle, war is vengeance; so that here men are punished for before breach of the King's laws in now the King's quarrel: where they feared the death they have borne life away, and where they would be safe they perish. Then, if they die unprovided, no more is the King guilty of their damnation than he was before guilty of those impieties for the which they are now visited. Every subject's duty is the King's, but every subject's soul is his own. Therefore should every soldier in the wars do as every sick man in his bed, wash every mote out of his conscience; and dying so, death is to him advantage; or not dying, the time was blessedly lost wherein such preparation was gained; and in him that escapes, it were not sin to think, that making God so free an offer, he let him outlive that day to see his greatness, and to teach others how they should prepare.

WILLIAMS: 'Tis certain, every man that dies ill, the ill upon his own head; the King is not to answer it.

Which of these arguments do you find convincing? What does it show about Hal that he argues so carefully – and that he feels he has to?

When Hal is alone again, he thinks about his responsibility:

HAL: Upon the King! 'Let us our lives, our souls,
Our debts, our careful wives,
Our children, and our sins lay on the King!'
We must bear all. O hard condition,
Twin-born with greatness, subject to the breath
Of every fool, whose sense no more can feel
But his own wringing! What infinite heart's ease
Must kings neglect that private men enjoy!
And what have kings that privates have not too,
Save ceremony, save general ceremony?
And what art thou, thou idle ceremony?
What kind of god art thou, that suffer'st more

Of mortal griefs than do thy worshippers?
What are thy rents? what are thy comings-in?
O ceremony, show me but thy worth!
What is thy soul, O adoration?
Art thou aught else but place, degree, and form,
Creating awe and fear in other men,
Wherein thou art less happy, being fear'd,
Than they in fearing?
What drink'st thou oft, instead of homage sweet,
But poison'd flattery? O, be sick, great greatness,
And bid thy ceremony give thee cure!
Think'st thou the fiery fever will go out
With titles blown from adulation?
Will it give place to flexure and low bending?
Canst thou, when thou command'st the beggar's knee,
Command the health of it? No, thou proud dream
That play'st so subtly with a king's repose,
I am a king that find thee, and I know
'Tis not the balm, the sceptre and the ball,
The sword, the mace, the crown imperial,
The intertissued robe of gold and pearl,
The farced title running 'fore the king,
The throne he sits on, nor the tide of pomp
That beats upon the high shore of this world,
No, not all these, thrice-gorgeous ceremony,
Not all these, laid in bed majestical,
Can sleep so soundly as the wretched slave,
Who with a body filled and vacant mind
Gets him to rest, crammed with distressful bread:
Never sees horrid night, the child of hell,
But, like a lackey, from the rise to set
Sweats in the eye of Phoebus, and all night
Sleeps in Elysium; next day after dawn
Doth rise and help Hyperion to his horse,
And follows so the ever-running year
With profitable labour to his grave.
And, but for ceremony, such a wretch,
Winding up days with toil and nights with sleep,
Had the fore-hand and vantage of a king.
The slave, a member of the country's peace,
Enjoys it, but in gross brain little wots
What watch the king keeps to maintain the peace,
Whose hours the peasant best advantages.

What new insights are offered here about the nature and the care of kingship?

There's enough here to show that the nature of kingship was a concern for Shakespeare in these plays. But the context is not only demonstrated by characters talking about it; these are plays, in which a range of characters speak, act and respond to each other's words and actions. To examine how the context appears, and what Shakespeare might be suggesting about it in these plays, you will find it helpful to look at some of the following:

- Hal's 'trial' of Falstaff at the end of Act 2 Scene 4 of *King Henry IV, Part 1,* and his actual rejection of him at the end of *Part 2.*

- The words spoken to Hal by his father in *Part 2,* rebuking him for his life-style.

- Hal's words in *Henry V* Act 1, in his dealings with the French Ambassador, and with the three traitors in Act 2 Scene 2.

- Hal's actions in the battles in *Henry V.*

- The words and behaviour of the French court – particularly the Dauphin, whose presentation makes the audience think further about the nature of kingship.

Another play that could provide material for a piece based on the context of kingship is *King Richard II*, where two different models are shown and discussed; the context is clear.

Gathering material about a conceptual context

In order to show fully how the context appears in the play you are studying, you need to look for evidence of some or all of these:

- What characters say directly about it, what characters do that reflects it, and how characters behave towards each other.

- How the context is shown in different episodes in the play – and often in sub-plots as well as the main action. In *Measure for Measure*, for instance, justice is clearly one of the central issues in the main action of the play, between Angelo and Isabella and the Duke; but it is also an issue in the sub-plots, too, which makes the audience reflect on the main plot in terms of the context of justice.

- What the playwright seems to be saying about the concept in the play. There may be several interpretations, of course, but your view will be based on the evidence you have found in going through the previous steps.

Writing the assignment, and extending to interpretations

As always, the key to writing successfully lies in the planning. When you've been through the steps above, you could choose a number of ways to structure the assignment. For example, you could follow the list above; you could start with a particular scene or exchange in the play where the context is clear, and move outwards from this; or you could start with a key line that expresses the concept in the play. However you decide to proceed, it's important to keep your eye on the concept and how Shakespeare uses a range of methods to make the audience think about it.

This type of assignment meets the Objectives about 'the contexts in which literary texts are written and understood' and 'knowledge and understanding'. You will have based your ideas on a careful consideration of the evidence in the text, and you'll have demonstrated this. The last step in the box suggests an 'independent judgement' too, but before you assume that you could meet all the Assessment Objectives in one 2,000 word piece, remember that the judgement has to be 'informed by different interpretations of literary texts by other readers'. You must consider how the concept could be interpreted in different ways as it appears in the text(s) you are studying.

Glossary

Allegory: an extended metaphor, usually a narrative or description which works on two levels simultaneously. It usually carries a hidden moral meaning; for example, George Orwell's *Animal Farm*.

Alliteration: a sequence of two or more words beginning with the same letter placed close together, for example: 'Full fathom five thy father lies'.

Ambiguity: occurs when it is possible to draw two or more meanings out of a literary work; for example, it is possible to read *Dr Faustus* as a warning about pride, or as a query about whether mankind may have such moral certainties as sin and redemption.

Archaic: the use of a word, phrase or style which is deliberately old-fashioned and no longer in popular use; for example the use of the word 'glebe' in Gray's *Elegy written in a Country Churchyard.*

Association: the range of meanings which a word has acquired which have a personal significance to the user. *See* **connotation**.

Assonance: the similarity of sound without actual rhyme, for example, 'Full fathom five thy father lies'.

Chivalric code: the rule of behaviour for knights in medieval times as defined in *The Romance of the Rose*, and evident as subject matter in Chaucer's writings.

Colloquial: informal language with familiar modes of speech as opposed to a formal use of language.

Conceit: a far-fetched comparison in which you are forced to admit likeness between two things, whilst always being aware of the oddness of the comparison. The Metaphysical poets were famed for their use of conceits, such as Donne's image of the compasses to describe two lovers.

Connotation: the extended significances of a word which are generally agreed: for example, purple is generally linked to royalty, mourning or Lent. *See* **association**.

Context: in AS Literary Studies this is the new fifth Assessment Objective. Contexts are the important facts, events or processes which have helped to shape literary works, for example, characteristics of contemporary styles.

Couplet: a pair of rhyming lines of verse.

Courtly love: the code of behaviour a knight must follow in courting his lady in medieval times. This was defined in *The Romance of the Rose*, and forms part of Chaucer's subject matter.

Cumulative process: a system that gathers meanings and associations.

Demonic: popular, colloquial or vulgar language.

Detached: used when a writer adopts an impartial view of things.

Dialect: a form of language which is specific to a person or district, in which there is a particular idiom, pronunciation or vocabulary. For example, 'Scouse' is the Liverpudlian dialect.

Dialogue: the part of literary works written as conversation.

Digression: a part of a literary work in which the writer appears to have drifted away from the main subject.

Double entendre: a phrase with two meanings, one of which is usually indecent, for example Wycherley's use of 'china' in *The Country Wife*.

Dramatic irony: a situation in drama where the audience knows more than the characters on stage.

Epilogue: the concluding part of a literary work in which originally the actors in a play addressed the audience; an author may address an epilogue at the end of a work to the reader, for example, Jane Austen's address to the reader at the end of *Mansfield Park*.

End-stopped rhyme: rhyming lines which contain a complete thought in each line.

Figurative language: language which contains figures of speech, for example, similes or metaphors.

Genre: a specific type or style of literature or art.

Half-rhyme: a type of verse in which the rhyme is not full, for example rhyme created by assonance. *See* **assonance**.

Heroic couplet: Iambic pentameters rhyming in pairs, famously used by Pope and Dryden, but also used by writers such as Chaucer and Keats. *See* **iambic pentameter**.

Iambic pentameter: a line of poetry with five weakly stressed syllables each followed by a strongly stressed syllabl, for example Shakespeare's

> When I do count the clock that tells the time.

Imagery: images used by a writer of poetry or prose in which a picture or sense-impression is conveyed in words.

Impressionistic: a style of writing in which impressions are conveyed by a non-realistic account of successive details, for example, the writing of Virginia Woolf and James Joyce.

Interior monologue: used when a writer conveys to the reader the thoughts of a character as they are being experienced.

Interlacing: part of the medieval principle of construction in which ideas are woven together intricately.

Internal rhyme: a line in poetry where there is rhyming inside the line.

Irony: present in writing or speech when the real meaning is concealed under language of the opposite meaning, often as a means of criticism; for example in the works of Jane Austen, Thomas Hardy and Jonathan Swift.

Metaphor: an implied or compressed comparison when one thing is said to take on the qualities of another, for example, Shakespeare's 'There's daggers in men's smiles.'

Metaphysical: a literary term invented by Dryden to describe a group of 17th century poets characterised by the use of far-fetched imagery and witty conceits. *See* **conceit**.

Miltonic: literary writings in the style of Milton; when used about the sonnet form this indicates a sonnet composed of an octet followed by a sestet. *See* **Petrarchan**, **octet** *and* **sestet**.

Motif: a dominant idea or image which re-appears throughout a work, such as the use of the colour red in *The Handmaid's Tale*.

Objective: the presentation of ideas uninfluenced by the writer's feelings or opinions.

Octet: in the sonnet form, the first eight-line section of a Miltonic sonnet.

Persona: assuming the role of a character in a play or literature.

Personification: the referring to an abstract idea in prose or poetry as though it were a person, for example Donne's address to death in his *Divine Sonnet*.

Petrarchan: the sonnet form originally created by Petrarch in the 14th century and later used by Milton, amongst others. *See* **Miltonic**.

Quatrain: a stanza of four lines, sometimes with alternate rhymes.

Register: a set of words used in specific circumstances, for example, in writing about war, a military register may be used by Wilfred Owen.

Satire: a literary work in which the aim is to amuse, criticise or correct by means of ridicule, for example the works of Jane Austen.

Sensual: related to the senses or sensations, usually with a sexual connotation rather than spiritual or intellectual.

Sensuous: appealing to the senses but with no restriction to fleshly or sexual pleasure.

Sestet: the second part of a Miltonic sonnet consisting of six lines.

Shakespearean sonnet: the sonnet form used by Shakespeare, consisting of three quatrains and a final summative couplet, or two rhyming lines.

Sibilance: a series of words with a hissing sound such as 's' and 'sh'.

Simile: a figure of speech using 'as' or 'like' in which there is a comparison used for clarity or vividness, for example Coleridge's 'as idle as a painted ship'.

Stanza: another name for a verse in a poem, with a set number of rhymes. The word comes from the Italian 'little room', as successive stanzas in a poem were seen to be like the rooms in a house, separate, but each leading out of one another.

Stream of consciousness: a literary style which follows, without obvious external structuring, the internal successive thought processes of a character, such as in the writings of Virginia Woolf and James Joyce.

Symbolism: a literary style originated in France in the 19th century in which the writer tries to create impressions rather than to describe things accurately.

Subjective: writing which aims to promote a personal point of view, and which is therefore not impartial.

Surrealism: writing in which things are presented as though perceived in a dream or in the subconscious mind, and not in a way which would seem to be realistic in an everyday way.

Syntax: the grammatical arrangement of words in writing or speech.

Theology: the science or study of religion, concerned with the knowledge of God.